THE COMPLETE GUIDE TO
INSPECTING, EVALUATING, AND BUYING RESIDENTIAL PROPERTY

THE COMPLETE GUIDE TO
INSPECTING, EVALUATING, AND BUYING RESIDENTIAL PROPERTY

**Become a knowledgeable home buyer. Avoid making a costly mistake.
Understand every element of the properties
you are considering before you sign a contract.**

JAMES E. BRIDGES & DEBORAH SPILLERS-BRIDGES

BETTERWAY PUBLICATIONS, INC.
WHITE HALL, VIRGINIA

Published by Betterway Publications, Inc.
P.O. Box 219
Crozet, VA 22932

Cover design by Deborah Chappell
Typography by TechType

Every precaution has been taken in preparing *The Complete Guide to Inspecting, Evaluating and Purchasing Residential Property* to make this book as complete and accurate as possible. Neither the authors nor Betterway Publications, Inc., however, assume any responsibility for any damages or losses incurred in conjunction with the use of this guide.

The following names used in this book are registered trademarks: Styrofoam®, Jenn-air®, Masonite®, Freon®, Sheetrock®, Formica®

Library of Congress Cataloging-in-Publication Data

Bridges, James E.
    The complete quide to inspecting, evaluating and purchasing residential property / James E. Bridges and Deborah Spillers-Bridges.
        p. cm.
    Includes index.
    ISBN 0-032620-91-4 (pbk.) : $9.95
    1. House buying. 2. Dwellings--Inspection. #. Dwellings--Valuation. I. Spillers-Bridge, Deborah. II. Title.
HD1379.b748 1988
643'.12--dc19   88-2886
                                                          CIP

Printed in the United States of America
0 9 8 7 6 5 4 3 2 1

DEDICATION

This book is dedicated to our children and grandchildren who make everyday worth living and remind us of the truly important things in life, to:

James E. Bridges, Jr., Jende Jane Bridges, Russ E. Bridges, Jodie Bridges-Preister, Russ D. Preister, Jodie Danielle Preister and Jessica Louise Preister.

Acknowledgements

We wish to thank the following professionals for their contributions of supportive information:

Steve Agid, Vice President, HMS Systems, San Francisco, CA.;
Claude S. Bridges, III, Vice President, Cecil Malone General Contractors, Atlanta, Georgia;
John C. Bridges, Builder, President, La Casa Concepts, Inc., Conyers, Georgia;
Wilson H. Hortman, Vice President, Elite Sales and Service,Inc.;
Andy Jelonnkiewicz, Vice President and Gary D. Marby, President, Underwriters,
Home Buyer's Warranty;
Mark Ozer; Jimmy Raven, Sales Rep.,R C Huddleston Concrete, Stockbridge, Georgia;
Lon J. Siebert, Manager, Lumber Division, Timber Products Inspection, Inc.;
Hoyt Swaney, Director of Permits and Licensing, Clayton County, Georgia;
Tim Williams, President, Williams Plumbing Contractors, Fayetteville, Georgia.

Table Of Contents

Introduction

The Complete Guide to Inspecting, Evaluating, and Purchasing Residential Property is exactly what the title indicates. Written in a conversational style, the book provides the homebuyer with almost all the know-how necessary to make an informed home selection decision. (Why "almost"? In a few critical circumstances, the home buyer is advised to seek the advice of a professional). Detailed checklists at the end of each chapter cover the house location and all aspects of the physical structure.

These checklists enable the prospective home buyer to "score" and compare as many as three houses being considered for purchase. In aggregate, they enable the buyer to rate each property on almost 200 individual characteristics; everything from neighborhood concerns (are changes in zoning regulations being contemplated?) to structural problems (are there any vertical cracks in the foundation?) to swimming pools (is the area surrounding the pool fenced?) and other amenities. Every point "scored" on a checklist indicates a current or potential, major or minor problem.

When an inspection has been completed, the prospective buyer is encouraged to total the scores on the master checklist provided at the back of the book. A combination of the scores recorded and the severity (cost to repair) of the problems identified should enable the buyer to make an informed decision about the house. The appropriate next step may be to walk away. It may be to make an offer? Or it may be to make an offer contingent on the owner or builder making necessary repairs.

Any major decision requires careful thought and consideration. That certainly applies to the purchase of a residential property. "Things often are not what they seem" is a truism that applies particularly to residential housing. Commercial builders usually work with trade unions. Each of these unions has an apprentice program, ensuring some measure of workmanship and quality control. However, speaking generally, the residential construction industry has no such unions. Except for the individual builder's reputation, no documented training or performance standards underpin the quality of the house being built.

There are few vocational schools that teach an individual how to become a home builder. And most of the tradesmen who do the flooring, roofing, sheetrock, etc., have no formal training. As a result, most residential tradesmen (subcontractors) learn through experience. In more real terms, by trial and error. Twenty years of experience in home building and real estate development has taught us many lessons. Lesson Number One? The quality of home construction is extremely variable.

Some construction mistakes may be obvious. Most of these can be corrected, many at relatively modest cost. Unfortunately there are mistakes that can be corrected only at great cost. The worst mistakes — those that can cause deep and continuing misery for the unenlightened home buyer — are the ones that go unnoticed, possibly because some cosmetic patching has concealed them.

Price does not insure quality. And component quality does not necessarily ensure house quality. For example a very expensive door can be hung improperly, causing frustration each time it is opened or closed. The door looks great but it functions poorly. And that makes a point that is repeated throughout the book: Try or test every door, every faucet, every appliance, etc.

The book will train you to look at every aspect of each house you are considering with eyes that see everything — on the surface and beneath the surface. If you are bothered by a symptom, you will be able to check, and understand, the cause. The whys of each condition are carefully explained. You will be taught to look beneath the

visible charm and appeal of the house to those materials and functions that give the house its intrinsic value — without minimizing the value of the finishing touches and amenities that make the house a home.

What things do you look for to determine the structural soundness of a new or previously occupied house? What kind of house are you really seeing? What kinds of problems have developed, or may develop in the future? What are the questions to ask and about what items?

It's impossible to know what influence today's decisions will have on our lives and finances tomorrow. We do know that, for most people, the decision to purchase a home is the most significant investment decision made in their lifetime. Clearly it is a decision that calls for the best informed, most prudent judgment possible. The intent of this book is to help you become that "best informed, most prudent" home buyer; to help you select the house that is right for you, because you have done your "homework".

1: The Lot and Neighborhood

When one looks at residential property — with a possible purchase in mind — he must first consider the site. In chapter one you are taken to the site and asked to scrutinize what you see at first glance. First impressions offer valuable insights; if something doesn't look right it probably isn't. Some information in this chapter is provided for the buyer who is having a house built. This information is given for guidance but it is limited and general, mostly referring to lot selection. Overall, both this chapter and the book address the existing house, whether it be a new or previously occupied home.

THE LOT

Houses are built on all kinds of lots: large, small, hilly, low, wooded, barren, etc. There is no answer to the question "Which lot is best?" because the decision actually depends upon personal preference. However, certain features make some lots poor choices. When the buyer knows these particulars he can make a wiser lot selection. For example, a low, marshy lot should be avoided. This type lot not only can cause the house to settle excessively, the lot stays wet most of the time.

The best lots demand the best price and of course the poorest lots cost the least. Sometimes, in an effort to build or buy in an exclusive neighborhood, a buyer purchases a "dog" lot thinking that

something can be done with it. In the process he finds that the cost to make the lot usable equals the price of the better lots. On occasion (with considerable professional advice) a poor lot can be a good buy, but the purchaser must be very well informed of the consequences. If you are in a position to purchase your own lot the most important consideration is the compatibility of the lot with your house plans. Professional advice from an engineer or architect is important if you are not a knowledgeable about construction.

Most of the time a homebuyer does not have the option of selecting the lot because houses are already built on the lot by the builder. The homebuyer needs to look at the house and the lot as a unit. No lot or house exists solely by itself. Every lot is connected to another lot, so lot choice also involves the lot's relationship to its neighbors. This relationship with respect to topography (the lay of the land), sewerage, traffic, taxes, etc. is discussed further in this chapter under surroundings.

LOCATION

When considering the location of a house certain questions arise. A family with small children wants to know the location of schools, playgrounds, and parks. People from out of town want to know about the closest shopping centers, churches, hospitals, and fire stations. Crime is a serious problem almost everywhere, so it would be to your advantage to know the kind and degree of criminal activity in the area you are considering.

The location of a house involves personal priorities. Some examples of these priorities are the choice of an hour's drive into town (and job) from the country, which you enjoy, or the convenience of intown living with its shorter commute but also fewer of life's more pleasing amenities — like trees. Another selection factor may be the importance of proximity to schools, public or private, or churches. If you are active in church, you could lose a half day a week to commuting time.

It is important to examine your lifestyle so you know what is important to you and what isn't and where time can be saved. Many times someone has said "I wouldn't have bought this far away from _____ had I known that I would spend half my life commuting." Sadly, this realization comes after the purchase of a home., when the cost and effort of the move have already been expended.

Another consideration might be sociability. Do you like being with people or do you prefer your solitude? If solitude is your preference then cluster housing is not a good choice but small acreage lots, which offer peace and quiet, may be just what you need. Priorities are as different as individuals, but there are homes and home sites available to meet everyone's needs. Inevitably, any home location selection will involve some compromises for you and other family members. Try to ensure that the decision-making process involves all the considerations that are important to you.

Perhaps the school system in the area in which you choose to live is particularly important to you. Schools are not created equal; some offer much more quality, variety, and depth in their programs than others. Some school systems provide programs for the handicapped, the learning-impaired and/or the gifted. Perhaps these same progressive systems are able to offer special programs in the arts and sciences. Across the country there are several schools geared specifically to the study of the performing arts; one such school is in the Atlanta Public School System, another in New York City.

What about the extracurricular activities ? These activities grow within the schools that make demands for them known and where there is support from the parents and community. It may be important to your children that a specific activity be available.

When you find the school that will meet the needs of your children you should make sure that your new home is located well inside the district lines for that school in the event that there should be any re-drawing of the lines. Will the school bus take your child to school? Usually, homes within close proximity of the school are not serviced by the buses. Do you need bus service so that you can leave for work earlier or later? How do you feel about your child(ren) walking to school? Some of these are relatively minor considerations but they could have a substantive effect on the lives of your children (what grade schooler, for example, wants to "commute" by school bus two hours a day?).

How important is the closeness of a hospital or rescue unit? What about the fire station (proximity could affect your home insurance rates)? For people with chronic illnesses a hospital in the immediate vicinity may be a necessity. Often it is the response time of the rescue unit that determines life or death. Someone who has already had one heart attack might want to consider this fact when choosing the location of the house. Is there a "911" service available in the area? Certain parts of the greater Atlanta area, for example, have had this service for many years; others are just recently benefitting from it.

For most of us, shopping does not have the same importance as schools and health facilities, but it is something to consider. What kinds of shopping do you and your family like to do? What are your favorite recreational activities? How about dining out or taking in the movies ? Will you be driving across town to take advantage of the facilities ? Most areas offer access to some basic shopping, like grocery stores and gas stations, but will you have to drive across town for the shops you enjoy? Not critical considerations perhaps, but they could affect the quality — and ease — of life you are seeking. And of course the time to think about them is before any purchase commitment is made.

Property values are also important when considering location. Have the values continued to rise or are they going down? Have the area's property values at least been stable? Prices rise and fall to some degree based upon supply and demand but the emphasis is placed on availability and the rate of interest. Age, location, and the economy of the area also affect property values. Examples of these factors are the rebirth of an old neighborhood through an urban renewal program, extension of a major interstate highway, and the opening or closing of a manufacturing plant. Property values are contingent on these and other considerations. It pays to watch what's happening in the area you are investigating. Be observant and ask lots of questions. When your investment and the way you and your family live are at stake, there is no such thing as a dumb question.

In any city or county, there are sections that have steady or greater than average rates of growth. Homes in these areas tend to be safe, sound investments. Many times there is a reputation that goes along with the area (e.g. the Governor's Mansion is the neighborhood centerpiece). Of course, higher prices usually accompany a neighborhood's reputation and prestige. Sometimes the same house in any other part of town will sell one-half the price. The track record of a given area is a good indicator of future trends but it is not a guarantee.

Few people know that fire insurance rates are based on a number of factors: distance from a fire hydrant, distance from a fire station, whether it is a paid or volunteer fire department, and water supply in the county or area. Therefore, someone living close to a fire station with proper water supply in the area would not pay the same for insurance as someone living in an area with no water lines and with a volunteer fire department. States set limits on maximum rates for fire insurance. Insurance companies can not deny insurance because of the situations mentioned above but the companies have the right to increase the premium for the policy. Proximity to both fire protection service and a water supply could be important if you are concerned about insurance costs and a (relatively) more safe fire protection environment.

SURROUNDINGS

Any lot is affected by the property around it. A major concern in developments is water. Where the water comes from and where it goes; for example, wells or city water, septic tanks or sewerage. Water control involves much more than the ease of turning water on and off.

If you look at a subdivision and try to imagine how it looked before it was developed you can see the ups and downs of the land, the topography. After the streets and houses are in place the water will flow the same as before with one exception; there will be more of it. The ground now covered with streets and houses can no longer absorb what it did before and the water becomes immediate runoff. The uncovered ground will absorb a percentage of the water but the excess inevitably becomes runoff. This runoff comes from rain in the area and from rain that occurs miles away at a higher elevation. Consequently, low lots have more water problems than higher ones. These factors are considered when the engineers survey the land and propose the site development. A number of problems can develop with low lots.

One piece of property that could have a runoff problem is the low lot that abuts a deadend street. When this lot is at the bottom of a hill the water running down the hill can jump the curb and run down the driveway or yard onto this lot and perhaps even into the house. This deadend lot (or the lot at the "bottom" of a cul-de-sac) will also have car lights shining into it. A similar situation is the low lot on a curve at the bottom of a hill. Again, excess runoff is likely.

Sewer drainage problems are more likely to happen with houses that are below street level. A serious situation occurs if a main line or manhole stops up. Since this lot is at a lower point on the sewer line, sewerage backs up into the house through the drain pipe. Sewer lines are placed in the ground and flow downwards to sewer treatment plants. In some cases a lift station (pumping station) is required to carry the waste to a higher location in order to obtain gravity flow to the treatment plant. The backup problem can also happen at the end of the line on low lots when the pumping station breaks down. Some building codes now require a backwash valve on the

sewer line entering the house on low lots allowing sewer drainage to flow in only one direction and not back into the house. If a low lot appeals to you, be sure to ask about back-up control measures.

Flood plans are projections that concern the possibility of flooding over a given period of time. There are twenty-five, fifty and one hundred year flood plans. How does the hundred year flood plan relate to your house or lot? A house does not need to be bordering a creek or river to be affected by high water. The probability of flood water is directly related to the height of your foundation and the flood plain in your area. Some municipalities require retention (detention) ponds to be installed in new developments. These ponds hold water that is the excessive runoff caused by the development. The object of the pond is to prevent water from flowing onto adjoining property at a greater rate after the development than before. This keeps the flood plain at the same elevation. Some subdivisions have oxidation ponds. These are small sewerage treatment plants serving only a given area. Don't mistake an oxidation pond for a small lake. Oxidation ponds and retention ponds are entirely different. Retention ponds are more common. Oxidation ponds have some type of equipment on the site to treat the sewerage.

Subdivisions at the end of main or major water or gas line are especially vulnerable to drops in pressure. Pressure drops can cause shortages, sometimes to the point where only dribbles of water are available for use. The prospective buyer can ask the builder or developer about shortages. Municipalities are obligated to tell the public about such complaints.

You also may want to check on the telephone and power companies to be sure that services are immediately available when you have bought a new house. In some situations — for instance a rapidly developing area — the final work for the subdivision is not completed by the utility company and there you may experience a short waiting period. You can call the utility companies to get this information.

Traffic flow can adversely effect the location and your life there, especially if the department of transportation decides to widen your street. Some beautiful residential properties have been ruined in the name of progress, so it is important to examine and understand the traffic situation, as it exists now and as it may change in the future. Where are the main streets and do you expect them to be widened? If you don't mind heavy traffic — fighting to get in and out of a driveway or having to protect small children — perhaps this isn't a problem. But if excessive traffic concerns you, you might want to locate further away from the main streets.

Taxes can increase dramatically in boom areas because growth is at a steady pace and new facilities like schools, water and sewerage treatment plants, and fire and police stations will need to be built or expanded, and staffed. If the old tax base will not support the growth, property tax increases are inevitable.

RESTRICTIONS

Most cities and counties have building and development restrictions. Some areas and circumstances have state restrictions. Subdivisions have their own restrictions which can be similar to or completely different from those of the municipalities. Subdivision restrictions are imposed by the developer and may last for twenty years or more. An example of a restriction may be the perimeter requirements of the front, side, and rear yards (building lines). Other restrictions impose limits on such matters as the ownership and free movement of pets, burning trash, and tree removal. The types of animals that may be kept (in some cases even the number of animals) may be restricted. Some restrictions cover trees, with approval required before a tree may be removed. Many counties require burning permits before trash or brush can be burned.

Most areas have building codes and standards. Newer construction and development standards may be more rigid as an area develops because previous circumstances manifest the need for upgrading. For example, fire hydrants may be closer together in a newer development than an older one. In some cases an occupancy certificate is required for both new and old houses when they are sold. This is a certificate issued by the building inspection department of the municipality which states that the house satisfies relevant codes. It allows utilities to be turned on without any additional work. In other words, the house is ready to occupy.

States normally have control in areas that affect adjacent towns, cities, or counties. Sewer disposal from a treatment plant into rivers and creeks is a good example because this water affects other localities further downstream. States control state highways and their right of ways. Sometimes states control the size of the lot that has a septic tank or well, even though the county enforces this requirement.

Subdivision restrictions can regulate almost anything, from the size of the house and lot to the placement and type of fencing. Many times the buyer must get approval of building plans not only for new construction but also for any room additions. The restrictions also can include the design and type of storage building (if any are allowed), and the use of part of the house for a business; for example beauty shop or day care nursery (which usually also requires a use permit). Historic districts normally have an additional set of restrictions. Within these historical areas prior approval by the neighborhood association may be required for such things as additions (like a storage building); even changing the exterior paint color. If you have ever been to a zoning meeting you know that such restrictions do exist. If you are contemplating any unusual alteration or application to the property you are proposing to purchase, you should check out all the restrictions that may apply.

HOUSE PLACEMENT ON THE LOT
Solar panels and room additions are affected by house placement. Solar panels need to be placed in a certain position to gain maximum efficiency from the sun. They can be placed on the front, back, or sides but obstructions (such as trees) will hinder efficiency. If you are thinking about using solar energy for heating and/or cooling, the position of the house and the obstructions around the house should be noted and considered.

Many times the homebuyer purchases a house with the intention of remodeling and making additions. Such alterations to an existing house require permits and approvals from the municipality. Often they also must meet subdivision covenants . Room additions and swimming pools are examples. If a room addition is anticipated then you need to know the restrictions and building lines because these will be the parameters of the addition. If the planned room addition is over the building lines a waiver or variance can sometimes be obtained from the city or county. This addition may still be subject to the restrictions of the subdivision even though the county approves. Building lines and easements (the right of use or passage across the property; e.g. overhead powerlines) are shown on a plat or survey.

The plat is available at the county courthouse and the survey may be obtained from the owner. However, an old plat or survey would not show any newly acquired easements. Information on a newly acquired easement is also found at the county courthouse. An example of a newly acquired easement would be the power company acquiring a new easement on the back of the property.

OUTSIDE DETAILS

All the things that you see from the curb as you first approach a house are outside details. From this viewpoint consider the things that may be a problem now or in the future. Perhaps the problem is purely cosmetic (you can't stand the color of the house so it will need to be repainted). It could be the traffic noise is horrendous. Or it could be a truly major problem, like the driveway exiting onto a blind curve.

As a buyer you should ask yourself, "what am I really seeing?" Is there anything that is or will be a problem for me? Try to visualize the house in different seasons and imagine what influence the weather will have on the house and lot. A lovely sloping driveway can be treacherous when coated with ice. Is ice a problem in your area? Ask the questions that are relevant to you. For example, are there any specific problems relating to yards and trees, drainage and washes, driveways and walkways?

YARD
Yards come in all configurations, with every variety of grasses, shrubs, and trees. They range from a manicured golf course look to rock gardens, where only pebbles grow.

Everyone enjoys a well-maintained lawn, but beautiful yards don't just happen. They are created by hard work and maintained, week after week, year after year. So, when looking at a lovely yard that someone has spent many hours grooming, you need to consider the time and money that it will take to keep it that way.

Is a lovely yard a priority on your time allotment card? Just watering the yard can be time-consuming. Is the sprinkler system manual or underground? It takes time to do it manually and installing automatic sprinklers certainly takes your money. Do you see any steep ups and downs to the yard? Are these steep places landscaped with grass or vines and groundcover? It is not safe to cut grass on steep inclines, even with a hand mower. If you are buying a new house and the lawn has just been planted, it will take time — and effort — to get it established.

Damp spots in the yard can mean many things: a simple low spot with poor drainage, a leak in an underground waterline, a septic tank needing attention, an underground spring, or a high water table. The water table is a level in the ground where water is normally found. This level moves up and down to some degree based upon rainfall and the season of the year. It would be wise to ask the owner if he knows the reason for the low spot so that you can rule out any unseen problems. You could ask if the situation happens all the time or only at certain times of the year. Consistency gives some hints to the cause of the problem. Most likely a constant presence indicates an underground spring or a waterline leak. Seasonal presence could mean a high water table or a septic tank problem.

TREES

Look at the trees on the lot. Do you like them? Would you remove any of them? Do any of them need to be removed out of necessity? What kind are they? Different trees thrive under different conditions. For example, poplar and willow trees thrive in Georgia, especially where there are underground springs and high water tables. High water tables and underground springs are of little concern unless you have a septic tank or a swimming pool, or plan to have a pool. Your county extension agent can tell you what trees to look for in your area that may indicate what the soil and water conditions are and may point to present or future problems.

An example of a tree that might need removal is one that is so close to the house that its root structure poses problems for the foundation. In time the roots of trees located around driveways can crack and lift up the paving, eventually requiring costly repaving. Are there any dead or dying trees? Dead trees are dangerous and should be removed. What is the cause for the condition? Might it affect other trees on the property? Who will remove the dead trees, you or the seller?

Mature but small trees may indicate rock on the property. The trees don't grow well around rock because the root system can not establish itself.Small trees can also mean poor soil conditions and/or lack of water. Does the neighbor's yard suffer from the same condition? You may want to ask the neighbor if he knows the cause. If rock is the suspected cause, further investigation is in order — particularly if you plan to add to the house or install an in-ground pool. Engineering firms can do "borings" which reveal the presence of rock and/or water but the procedure is costly. Rock removal is expensive. (Rock involvement is covered further in chapter two, under foundations and footings).

Trees and powerlines can be a dangerous combination. Are your powerlines overhead or underground? Power can be lost in storms by trees falling on powerlines. A house with underground power does not have this problem or the dangers associated with fallen powerlines. However, since most houses have overhead service (probably including the one you plan to buy), it would be wise to purchase a wooden or fiberglass ladder for any repairs near the lines. There have been many accidents and a number of deaths caused by aluminum ladders touching overhead powerlines.

DRAINAGE

Most houses have swales in the yards. Swales are man-made low places around the house and lot lines. They are designed to carry water downhill to drainage ditches or pipes. Swales are intended to keep the water away from the house and to eliminate puddles. When these swales on the side and back of the lot are recorded on surveys or subdivision plats they are called drainage easements. This means that water from surrounding lots has the assigned right to flow across your yard. You can not disturb the flow. The flow is established by an engineer's study which is county approved.

A drainage pipe does not need to be present on your lot for you to have a drainage easement. Drainage easements can be swales in the yard or pipes in the ground. Low lots get the runoff from higher lots, so if your lot is lower than the adjacent lot, chances are you have a drainage easement (probably at the back of the lot). Water flows down the drainage easements to drainage pipes which are located at the back or side property lines of the lot. Then, drainage pipes carry the water under the streets or to a lower location. The size of the drainage pipe is a good indication of the amount of water drainage to anticipate.

The worst situation involving drainage is the house on a low lot that has the following: street level higher than the first level of the house, a drainage pipe on the lot, sides lots that are higher and the back lot that is higher. If the drainage pipe stops up the water must rise to street level in order to go to a lower location and therefore the house would flood. If this situation exists you probably would want to reject that particular house.

Washes and ditches indicate that water flows across the yard at these locations. The size of either is directly related to the amount of water coming across the yard. Small washes and ditches may simply mean that the owner neglected the yard. It is very hard to establish a yard with extensive water drainage because the water keeps washing the grass seed away before a root system can be established. With extensive ditches and washes you may want to seek the advice of a landscape architect.

DRIVEWAYS/WALKWAYS/PATIOS

Driveways can be made from concrete, asphalt, brick, or other materials. The difference in the materials makes a difference in the quality of the driveway. One example is concrete; it comes in different strengths and steel reinforcement may or may not be used. Asphalt comes in many types, too. There are different thicknesses of concrete and asphalt. Just as important as the visible surface of the driveway is the content underneath (subgrade). The dirt should have been well compacted and dry. Look at the driveway. Do you see large cracks? Is the driveway separating? Such conditions may indicate that the subgrade was handled improperly. In most such cases the driveway eventually will need to be replaced. However, not all driveway problems are construction problems. Residential drives are not made to support more than normal weight loads. (Other physical factors involved with problem driveways are discussed in chapter two, under foundations and concrete).

Another entirely different aspect concerning driveways is safety. When entering or leaving the driveway can you see clearly in both directions? Under all weather conditions? Is the driveway wide enough for easy access? Does the car drag going in or out? What about adverse weather conditions? In ice and snow conditions, steep driveways can leave residents stranded.

Depending on your lifestyle, patios and walkways can be important. Will you be using the patio for cookouts on a regular basis? Or do you prefer to grill inside? These questions make a difference because they are your priorities. If you use the patio regularly then it would certainly be a annoyance to have puddles of water standing for days because of poor concrete work. Putting up with a sloping patio or walkway also could be irritating. Poor weather conditions would only make matters worse.

APPEARANCE

The outside appearance of a house speaks volumes to the potential buyer. A well kept house and neighborhood reflect in property values. Conversely, other conditions can have an adverse effect on values. As you drive through the area do you see more "for sale" signs than in other areas? If so, find out why. Was land nearby recently rezoned for apartments? For commercial development? Do you see signs of encroaching urban blight around the periphery of the area?

Basically there are two types of houses: attached and detached. The detached house is a single unit built on a lot by itself. Maintenance and upkeep are the sole responsibility of the owner. The attached house includes the condominium and townhouse. The condominium has common area, like a swimming pool and tennis courts, which is maintained by an association that oversees the work. Fees are paid by the owners to the association. A townhouse is defined as having a small individual yard, cared for by the owner, and being attached to other townhouses. Townhouses also may have common areas. If the townhouse has a common area, the maintenance system is very much like that in a condominium association.

Are the condominium grounds well kept? Well kept grounds suggest a well managed association. Poorly maintained grounds perhaps are telling you the staff has been cut to meet the association's budget. The association fees are subject to increase because of inflation. In some cases the fees have risen to nearly equal the mortgage payment. How many increases in association fees have there been in the past five years? Condominium insurance is different because one policy covers the buildings and a separate policy, which is similar to a renter's policy, covers personal contents. Part of the association fees covers the cost of the group policy. As rates go up the association may choose to adjust the policy. Some items(for example, frozen pipe coverage) may be dropped from the policy in an effort to cut expenses. If you are planning a condominium purchase, be sure the policy coverage is adequate.

When an excessive number of units are for sale in the same project it can mean many things: that there are structural problems which are unresolved; commonly metered water and sewer connections with equal bills regardless of the owner's use; water pipes freezing each year without coverage; poor insulation causing excessive power bills; increase in association fees to cover accumulating repairs; or basically a mismanaged association. Usually, house prices are based on supply and demand but there can be other reasons like those just mentioned. If a condominium or house is not priced at a level comparable to similar homes in the area, you should investigate the reasons for the price difference. What does the seller know that you don't? Someone may be trying to unload a problem at your expense.

When you are looking at the outside appearance of a single family dwelling the same factors apply. When a house is new you are seeing it at its best. As time goes by, elements need to be painted, repaired, or replaced. Is the house in good repair or does it look as though it has been unevenly maintained? When a section of the roof is a different shade it can mean that the roof has been patched in one spot only, rather than completely reroofed. If the house has been repainted, has some rotting siding been cosmetically concealed? These boards should have been replaced. If corners have been cut where you can see them it is likely they also have been cut where the results are not visible.

EXPLANATION FOR USE OF THE CHECKLIST

Each checklist in this book is designed somewhat like a golf scorecard; i.e., the lowest score wins.Since any point is an implicit negative, the house you want should not have accumulated very many. The checklist is a simple but invaluable tool. You probably will want to compare at least three houses, so each chapter includes three checklists. Copies can be made if more are needed.

Each question asked on the list has been covered in the preceding chapter. If any question is unclear you can refer back to the text. The scoring of a question should be easy if you know the answer. However, a problem may arise when you are in doubt. This is the reason for the "HOLD" column. Any question that you are unable to answer will require further investigation. Just check "HOLD" until you get an answer. Once you have the answer you can score the question. The accumulative score is transferred to the "MASTER CHECKLIST" at the back of the book.

Any house that has scored a check in the "MAJOR" column needs careful consideration and probably professional advice. A major item is anything that either will take thousands of dollars to remedy or is not feasible at all to correct. A major check is intended to be a warning to the homebuyer and additional information on it should be listed in "REMARKS". Further scrutiny and comparison "REMARKS" should include your comments on the money, time, and complications involved in dealing with a major problem.

The "OTHERS" portion of "REMARKS or OTHERS" gives you the option of listing any personal statements that are pertinent to the checklist. Additional room is provided on the back of the checklist page.

Checklist #1: The Lot and Neighborhood

	House #1 Location:_____	NO PROBLEM	MINIMUM	MINOR	MAJOR	HOLD
		0	1	2	3	?
1	Are you pleased with the lot?					
2	Will the lot require extensive work?					
3	Does the location of the house satisfy your priorities?					
4	Are property values consistent with comparable neighborhoods?					
5	Will the distance from the fire station present any problems?					
6	Is the lot below street level? Any potential problems?					
7	Have there been any problems with sewer backup?					
8	Is the house situated at the end of water or gas main lines?					
9	Are there any unforeseen adverse neighborhood developments?					
10	What is the probability of a property tax increase?					
11	Will any current/anticipated zoning restriction affect your plans?					
12	Is a certificate of occupancy required?					
13	Will compliance with subdivision restrictions be a problem?					
14	Do you plan using solar energy? Any anticipated problems?					
15	Are there any obstacles concerning remodeling?					
16	Do yard maintenance requirements comply with your lifestyle and needs?					
17	Have there been any water problems with the yard?					
18	Will tree removal be necessary?					
19	Are any ditches or washes causing trouble?					
20	Are rock formations or ledgescausing any problems on the lot?					
21	Are there drainage problems on the lot or with the house?					
22	Does the driveway need repair?					
23	Are there any driveway safety considerations?					
24	Is the neighborhood stable?					
25	Have the grounds been well maintained?					
26	If condominium: Do the grounds and facilities appear well maintained?					
27	Condominiums or houses: Has there been a high number of resales?					
28	REMARKS OR OTHER:					
29						
30						

**TRANSFER SUB-TOTALS TO
MASTER CHECKLIST FORM**

SUB-TOTAL

ADDITIONAL REMARKS OR OTHERS:

Checklist #1: The Lot and Neighborhood

	House #2 Location:_____	NO PROBLEM	MINIMUM	MINOR	MAJOR	HOLD
		0	1	2	3	?
1	Are you pleased with the lot?					
2	Will the lot require extensive work?					
3	Does the location of the house satisfy your priorities?					
4	Are property values consistent with comparable neighborhoods?					
5	Will the distance from the fire station present any problems?					
6	Is the lot below street level? Any potential problems?					
7	Have there been any problems with sewer backup?					
8	Is the house situated at the end of water or gas main lines?					
9	Are there any unforeseen adverse neighborhood developments?					
10	What is the probability of a property tax increase?					
11	Will any current/anticipated zoning restriction affect your plans?					
12	Is a certificate of occupancy required?					
13	Will compliance with subdivision restrictions be a problem?					
14	Do you plan using solar energy? Any anticipated problems?					
15	Are there any obstacles concerning remodeling?					
16	Do yard maintenance requirements comply with your lifestyle and needs?					
17	Have there been any water problems with the yard?					
18	Will tree removal be necessary?					
19	Are any ditches or washes causing trouble?					
20	Are rock formations or ledgescausing any problems on the lot?					
21	Are there drainage problems on the lot or with the house?					
22	Does the driveway need repair?					
23	Are there any driveway safety considerations?					
24	Is the neighborhood stable?					
25	Have the grounds been well maintained?					
26	If condominium: Do the grounds and facilities appear well maintained?					
27	Condominiums or houses: Has there been a high number of resales?					
28	REMARKS OR OTHER:					
29						
30						

TRANSFER SUB-TOTALS TO
MASTER CHECKLIST FORM   SUB-TOTAL

ADDITIONAL REMARKS OR OTHERS:

_____

_____

_____

_____

_____

_____

_____

_____

_____

_____

_____

_____

_____

Checklist #1: The Lot and Neighborhood

	House #3	NO PROBLEM	MINIMUM	MINOR	MAJOR	HOLD
	Location:_____	0	1	2	3	?
1	Are you pleased with the lot?					
2	Will the lot require extensive work?					
3	Does the location of the house satisfy your priorities?					
4	Are property values consistent with comparable neighborhoods?					
5	Will the distance from the fire station present any problems?					
6	Is the lot below street level? Any potential problems?					
7	Have there been any problems with sewer backup?					
8	Is the house situated at the end of water or gas main lines?					
9	Are there any unforeseen adverse neighborhood developments?					
10	What is the probability of a property tax increase?					
11	Will any current/anticipated zoning restriction affect your plans?					
12	Is a certificate of occupancy required?					
13	Will compliance with subdivision restrictions be a problem?					
14	Do you plan using solar energy? Any anticipated problems?					
15	Are there any obstacles concerning remodeling?					
16	Do yard maintenance requirements comply with your lifestyle and needs?					
17	Have there been any water problems with the yard?					
18	Will tree removal be necessary?					
19	Are any ditches or washes causing trouble?					
20	Are rock formations or ledgescausing any problems on the lot?					
21	Are there drainage problems on the lot or with the house?					
22	Does the driveway need repair?					
23	Are there any driveway safety considerations?					
24	Is the neighborhood stable?					
25	Have the grounds been well maintained?					
26	If condominium: Do the grounds and facilities appear well maintained?					
27	Condominiums or houses: Has there been a high number of resales?					
28	REMARKS OR OTHER:					
29						
30						

TRANSFER SUB-TOTALS TO
MASTER CHECKLIST FORM

| SUB-TOTAL | | | | |

ADDITIONAL REMARKS OR OTHERS:

2: Basic Structural Elements, Foundation, and Framing

Chapter two examines the structure of both foundations and framing. As you read through this chapter you will notice that there are no diagrams or pictures. This book will not attempt to teach you how to interpret two dimensional drawings; these are limited in scope and can not accurately depict problems. The intent is to teach you the reasons behind certain problems; for example, a cracked foundation. A picture can show a crack in the foundation but it will not explain what caused the crack. As the chapter continues to explain differences in cause and effect you learn to determine the extent and correction of the problems. Unfortunately, you soon learn that one problem often leads to another.

Most municipalities have minimum building codes. These codes do not guarantee quality, in fact, minimum standards only set minimum requirements. Understanding the difference between cost effective building and " cutting corners " building is important to you. Communicating that understanding is another purpose of this book.

THE FOUNDATION

The foundation is the main support of a house. There are two parts to a foundation, the footing and some type of structured foundation wall. A proper foundation is vital because virtually everything else is dependent "upon" it. The foundation is not the only component that can have structural damage, but since this book deals with the house from the ground up, it is the first matter to be addressed. If the foundation cracks and/or settles, causing movement of the foundation, the house structure will move with it. Because of their basic importance, much of this chapter addresses the problems associated with poorly constructed foundations.

FOOTINGS

Although the footing of an existing house cannot be seen, it probably is the most important element in the structural soundness of a house. Footings, the "foundation" of the foundation, are the main support for the entire weight load of the house. If the footings are not constructed properly, everything else can be done correctly and the house still can have problems.

Footings are trenches dug into the ground, then filled with concrete. When the house is completed dirt is pushed up against the footing and foundation wall. This protects the ground underneath the footing against freezing, which would loosen the ground and cause settlement.

For this same reason, footings are placed in the ground below the frostline, the lowest depth in the ground to which freezing is expected.

The only time a buyer could see the footing would be during the building of the house, but evidence of a footing problem can be seen by checking the foundation wall for vertical cracks. Certain factors determine the ability of the footing to do the proper job. These factors are: type of soil in the area, the compaction of the ground beneath the footing, the depth of the footing in the ground (frostline), the thickness and width of the footing, the strength of the concrete, and the use of steel reinforcement. If the footings fail, the house will settle unevenly and cracks will appear in the foundation wall. In an area with expanding soil conditions (Denver, for example), the opposite may happen. The footing may rise up rather than settle. In extreme cases, cracks show up in the interior and exterior walls of the house. The width, length, and direction of the crack reveal clues as to the cause. When a crack occurs because the ground was not compacted properly, the house will continue to settle and crack until the ground is sufficiently compacted. This settling can continue for years, and the cracks will continue to expand and lengthen.

THE FOUNDATION WALL

Today, most foundation walls are either concrete block or poured in place concrete. Foundation walls also are made of brick, rock, or granite. In recent years there has been an increased use of pressure treated wood as a foundation wall. However, the wood foundation may have a limited life expectancy. In northern states, wood foundations have been in the ground for twenty years or more, with no problems reported. Some authorities believe a wood foundation has a lifespan equal to concrete products, but, as of this writing, that foundation has not been adequately

time tested. When you consider that thirty years is a typical term for a home mortgage, you may want to think over very carefully buying the kind of structure that may present problems toward the end of that term.

All houses settle to some degree, even if it is only minutely. This action occurs naturally as an adjustment of the structure to the ground. A properly constructed foundation will settle evenly, but it still may show hairline cracks (these can occur in the best of foundations). In fact, the nationwide Home Buyers Warranty program state their construction standard as:

"Non-structural cracks are not unusual in concrete foundation walls. Such cracks greater than 1/8 inch are considered excessive. The builder shall repair non-structural cracks in excess of 1/8 inch. Surface patching is acceptable for non-structural cracks."

Stress cracks differ from non-structural cracks, and are signs of possible structural problems. There are two types of vertical stress cracks in foundation walls. One begins and is largest at the bottom of the foundation wall and the other has its largest gap at the top. Sometimes when the crack is largest at the bottom, it means that the footing has settled excessively at that point and caused the foundation wall to crack. In some parts of the country this can occur when the soil expands. The foundation can be pushed up and develop cracks. This settlement crack can begin to pull the foundation apart from underneath, with a pulling down effect. If it is detected in time, the situation can be corrected by reinforcement.

When the crack is largest at the top, there already has been some settlement. One side of the house is settling more than another. The corrections called for depend on the extent of the damage;

they may require leveling of the house and reinforcing the footing. The primary way to halt settlement cracks is to go under the problem; that is, to provide adequate support beneath the footing or foundation wall. This is a costly and difficult procedure. Unless the purchase price of the house is low enough to reflect the magnitude and repair cost of this problem, the prospective buyer should look for his dream house elsewhere.

With this information in mind, you can begin to examine the foundation of the house. Ideally you will not find cracks in the foundation. Uneven settling causes vertical cracks which indicate some degree of stress. The degree of stress involvement is directly related to the load bearing capacity of the ground (stability) that supports the structure and to the design of the footing and foundation wall which should carry and distribute the weight load evenly. Cracks are more likely to be seen where the weight loads change. An example is the point at which the two story part of a house joins the one story part.

Remodeling can cause stress cracks when additional weight is brought to bear on a foundation that was not intended to handle more than the original load. The amount of "misdirected" settlement is reflected in the direction and size of the stress cracks. Together, the size and direction of the cracks determine the structural soundness of the foundation. In virtually all cases, stress cracks appearing inside the house are cause for alarm, particularly in a newer house. This condition, by itself, is enough reason to either seek professional advice or walk away.

CONCRETE

Concrete is a mix of cement, sand, and gravel. The main purpose of concrete is to act as a structural support. It is the support element for the foundation of the house. Concrete comes in different strengths for different applications. Steel reinforcement rods may be added for additional strength. The requirements of the job determine the strength of the concrete and the use of reinforcement rods, if necessary.

When wire mesh is used, it acts as a bonding agent rather than adding structural strength. Its purpose is to hold or stabilize the concrete. If a driveway begins to crack from settlement, the wire mesh would prevent one side of the crack from settling lower than the other, at the same time minimizing the width of the crack. Concrete will not bond to concrete unless it is all poured at the same time, while still loose or wet.

Expansion joints are man-made. They are necessary in concrete work because concrete expands and contracts with changes in temperature. If expansion joints are not present, or are insufficient in number, unplanned expansion cracks will develop. Expansion cracks are non-structural, hairline cracks that run in a relatively straight line. Expansion cracks normally appear in carports, garages, driveways, large patios, and some basements. Settlement cracks, however, tend to be larger and start in one direction — then may change course. Again, the Home Buyer's Warranty states:

"Concrete slabs within the structure are designed to move and settle at expansion and contraction joints. Movements caused by expansion and contraction may cause cracks and voids to appear in the slab."

Sometimes when concrete is drying curing cracks appear. These are hairline cracks on the surface of the concrete. Curing cracks look very much like the fine lines on an egg shell. They do not always occur, but when they do they are of no concern. They merely indicate an adjustment of the drying concrete to the weather conditions at the time and the procedure used.

Concrete work is finished in two ways. A trowel finish is very smooth. It is used mainly in basements, garages, house slabs, and some carports. A broom finish is used for driveways, walkways, steps, porches, patios, and some carports. The broom, or brushed, surface provides a safety measure, in that it is not as slippery as the trowel finish. If, when you sweep the concrete, you repeatedly produce a powdery, sandy residue, it probably means the concrete froze before it was able to set (dry) or it is a defective concrete mix. Another cause for this condition can be improper procedure; e.g., too much water added to the concrete while it was being worked into place. In either case, the concrete will need to be replaced or resurfaced because it is apt to continue to disintegrate.

The weather affects concrete work during the construction stage and continually thereafter. This is especially true of any concrete work which is constantly exposed to the elements. The most common example is a cracked driveway. When water seeps into the crack the ground underneath is loosened. When a heavy weight is applied, therefore, settlement will occur. Matters are made worse if the water should freeze. Driveway cracks should be filled as soon as they are noticed. The filling should be appropriate to the composition of the driveway; a concrete caulk for concrete, an asphalt caulk for an asphalt driveway.

If the top of the concrete finish is flaking off in small pieces, this probably means the concrete work has been resurfaced. Resurfacing is applied on top of a poorly finished concrete job to improve it. Usually the repair is made by applying cement, a component of concrete, over the top of the concrete. However, the cement will not con-

tinue to adhere over any length of time, and flaking will result. Pitting of the concrete occurs when the surface loosens, leaving tiny holes. This situation also can happen with resurfacing or with too much water being added to the mix during the construction stage (too much water weakens the mix). Other causes of pitting are improper concrete mix from the plant (e.g., too much sand and not enough cement) and rain falling before the concrete has dried.

There are products on the market that will bond to concrete so that the problem area can be resurfaced satisfactorily. However, these products will not bond to concrete that has been frozen unless the damaged concrete has been removed. Severely damaged driveways — those with the ground showing through — require special attention. In most cases, the only solution is to remove and replace the damaged sections.

CRAWL SPACE

The crawl space is the area under a house between the ground and the bottom of the floor system. As its name implies, it allows room to crawl but not to stand. If a house has a crawl space, a prospective buyer can learn a lot about the soundness of the house by looking into the crawl space area. A powerful flashlight will be very useful for those who do not wish to crawl in.

Cracks in the foundation walls may be patched and hardly noticeable from the outside of the house. From the crawl space, however, the cracks probably are quite visible. Rarely does anyone patch both sides of a foundation crack. Any wood that has been replaced or added in the floor system also is more visible from within. Termites or rotted wood might be the cause for the replacement. You will want to know the reason. Ask the "why and what" questions to ensure, to your satisfaction, that the problem was fixed . . . not merely patched.

Piers are present when there is a crawl space. They rest on a footing and support the house's structure. Piers are either steel or masonry columns. Masonry piers can be checked for cracks; they will look like those described in the section on foundation walls. New piers would indicate some previous need for additional support (perhaps for weight added by remodeling). If you learn that the house has been remodeled, you should be reassured to know that extra measures were taken to maintain the structural soundness of the house.

The crawl space area also has water and drain pipes that are exposed. In most houses with crawl spaces, the electrical wiring and heat ducts are also present in that area. All of these can be checked for obvious flaws or alterations. The specific conditions to look for are described in Chapter Four.

SLAB

A house built on a slab is one built on a concrete floor. Slabs normally are supported by the ground. However, a slab also can be constructed to be free standing, supported by columns or piers. Most commercial buildings have free standing slabs while most slab houses are ground supported.

A house with a slab foundation, supported by the ground, still has piers and grade beams, which are concrete footings under the slab for support. If a slab cracks and settles, it cannot be jacked up to a level position, as could be done for a house with a wooden floor system over a crawl space. The slab would need to be redone or properly resurfaced to correct the problem.

Typically, a house built on a slab has both a living area and an exposed area (often a carport). The living area should have gravel and polyurethane (plastic film) under the slab. These help

prevent moisture from being drawn up through the slab. If the gravel and plastic film have not been used, the house may have a damp, musty smell. Also, any flooring applied with adhesive may pull loose. The floor could actually feel damp. Sealing the slab after the fact may help, but it will not eliminate the problem.

Where the slab is covered with carpet or tile, you will want to feel for high and low spots as you walk across each room. Changes in the floor levels may have been caused at the time of construction, when the concrete was poured, or by settlement afterward. Unless the house has other signs that point to a settlement problem, (like cracks in the foundation), slight variations in the floor are non-structural and there is no real cause for alarm.

When you examine the exposed areas — the carport, for example — do you see any low spots, water stains, cracks, or areas of settlement? If this area is to remain exposed, the extent of any problem you discover will determine the need for repair. However, if you intend to use the exposed area for future expansion of the living area (maybe converting the carport to a TV room) it will need to be leveled. Since this area has not been prepped with gravel and polyurethane you would have to use a masonry floor product, like slate or ceramic tile, to prevent the problems just mentioned.

This statement from the Home Buyer's Warranty should help you judge problems with a slab:

"Concrete floors in basements or rooms designed for habitability should not have pits, depressions, or areas of unevenness that would prevent their use as finished floors. The floor slope, unless designed for specific drainage purposes, shall not exceed 1/240th of the room width.

Cracks in garage slabs in excess of 1/4 inch in width or 1/4 inch in vertical displacement are considered excessive and unacceptable (not referring to man-made expansion joints)."

A hairline horizontal crack in a block foundation that abuts a concrete slab usually is an expansion crack, the result of the slab expanding and contracting. You will want to be sure that the foundation wall has not moved in towards or out from the house. That would indicate a structural problem; the wall would not be holding or supporting what is intended.

Newer slab built houses may have perimeter insulation of styrofoam or other sheet type insulation. It is placed under the slab, at the outside edges, during construction. An alternate approach is placing the sheeting on the outside foundation wall before backfilling. The purpose of the insulation is to prevent the radiating temperature, on freezing days, from coming through the slab. It also protects the water pipes on the perimeter of the house from freezing.

BASEMENT

The exterior walls of a basement also are the foundation walls of the house. Always the lowest level or floor of a house, a basement usually is left unfinished by the builder. Often it is finished at a later date by the occupant, with a game or "rec" room the most common result. If the basement of the house you are inspecting has not been finished, the exposed foundation walls and floor system can tell you a lot about the structural soundness of the house.

Look for any obvious curves or bows in the foundation wall. They might indicate excessive weight being applied to that area. At worst, a bowed (inward) wall could mean that too much dirt or other assorted material (some builders use the excavation area outside the foundation walls as a "dumping ground" for leftover cement and other heavy matter) is pushing the wall in. Occasionally the foundation wall is backfilled while it is still "green", before it has set or dried. That latent weakness could cause the wall to give. Sometimes a bowed wall is merely the result of poor masonry work.

Those with qualified opinions in this area are more concerned with a new house with a bowed foundation wall than they are with a twenty year old house that has a slightly curved basement wall but shows no signs of other foundation problems.

When you are in the basement, feel the walls for possible dampness. If dampness exists, it indicates slow seepage of water through the concrete block or poured foundation. All basement walls will feel cool, but dampness should give you cause for concern. Slow seepage is different from a leak — water trickling or flowing into a basement. A leak is obvious, but may be detectable only during or after a heavy rain.

Any dampness or leakage problem should be corrected. Application of a waterproofing product designed for interior wall application may solve the dampness problem. A leak, however, will require more serious (expensive) repair work, possibly including exterior waterproofing.

Most houses with basements have a foundation drain system; gravel and pipe that lead the water away from the house. If such a system was not built into the house you are considering, it may have to be done to alleviate present — or forestall future — problems.

RETAINING WALLS

Retaining walls are used primarily for functional

purposes, but often they add a decorative touch as well. An example would be terracing down a slope, each wall installed to keep the ground behind it from washing away. Retaining walls are constructed from concrete block, other concrete products, brick, and treated wood (most commonly, railroad or landscaping ties).

A masonry wall should have the longest productive life. It should have "weep" holes near the bottom of the wall; these allow the water to seep through during or after a heavy or prolonged rain. A very heavy rain will create enough hydrostatic pressure to cause a masonry wall without "weep" holes to collapse.

If a retaining wall is bowing, it is not doing its job effectively and should be reconstructed or replaced. Cracks would also indicate that the wall is in danger of giving way. Referring to the Foundation section on cracks will help you determine the type and severity of the cracks.

If the retaining wall is not constructed of masonry, you may find wood that is rotting. Not only does that indicate a wall in danger of failure, it indicates a landscaping feature that is cosmetically unattractive.

THE FRAME (FRAMING)

The frame — or framing, as it is more commonly called — is the skeleton of the house. It is the essential structure to which everything else is applied. There are many kinds and sizes of lumber used in framing a house, each used for a particular reason. When there is a problem with the framing (for example, a floor that bows or a ceiling that sags), it is likely that the appropriate size and/or type lumber was not used and that what was substituted is unable to support the weight load.

Two terms are used to describe weight loads for construction: "dead load", the weight applied to the frame of the house as it is built; and "live load", the weight of everything that occupies the house. The "live load" includes people, furniture, even the snow on the roof. A house must be designed and constructed to support both loads. The fact that different living areas in the house are expected to carry different weight loads also must be reflected. The kitchen and family rooms carry more weight because people tend to congregate in those areas.

Also be mindful of the ages of the houses you are comparing. A new house has yet to go through the stages it probably will go through as it "matures". An older house, on the other hand, has matured; like most people, it has settled a bit here, wrinkled a bit there. You probably are seeing it at its worst. You are not apt to see any additional deterioration unless the house had been added to or significant remodeling has been done. For example, a foundation crack in a house that is twenty years old probably will not widen or deepen. The same crack in a one year old house might be cause for concern.

FLOORS

Floors have two component parts before the covering is applied; the floor system or joist, and the sub-flooring. The sub-flooring usually is plywood, installed on top of the floor joist. The finished flooring, the hardwood, tile, carpeting, etc.,is then installed on top of the sub-flooring.

Because normal vibrations, over time, will loosen the sub-flooring, most houses have or will develop floor squeaks. The areas of the house with the most traffic tend to develop squeaks first. The better the entire floor system has been constructed to carry the weight load, the less likely the floor is to develop squeaks.

Floors should be level. Levelness is a condition that is easily checked. Simply place a marble on the hardwood or tile floor. If it rolls, the floor is not level. If it rolls swiftly, the problem is more severe. If the floor is carpeted, you can check levelness with a carpenter's level, in both directions and at several locations.

The most common reason for a floor that is not level is a basic one; the house was not built level. Every piece of lumber has a crown. The crown can be a slight to very noticeable rise in the wood. In construction, the crown of the wood is placed up to take on the weight. When this is not done, problems can occur. An excessive crown can cause a bump in the floor. That same piece turned downward can cause a dip in the floor. Either way, that particular piece of wood should not have been used and correction may require replacement.

The following statement from The Home Buyer's Warranty booklet tells you the extent to which a floor can be out of level:

"Floors should not be more than 1/4 inch out of level within any 32 inch horizontal measure. Floor slope within any room shall not exceed 1/240th of the room width. Allowable floor and ceiling joist deflections are governed by the approved building code."

Checking the floors for abnormal vibrations is one of the best ways to assess the structural integrity of a floor system. If the floor system is solid, the vibrations should be minimal. Normal walking should not produce any vibrations or movement of any items on or near furniture. You might also want to stand on your toes, then drop to your heels. That impact will ripple through the floor system and produce vibrations. If the system is sound, any vibrations felt should be slight.

Excessive settlement of the house can also cause out of level floors. If settlement is the cause, that will involve more than just the floors and could be a matter of serious concern. There probably is no reason to be concerned with a minor squeak here and there, but when floor squeaks are accompanied by other signals — like a cracked foundation and floors that literally "bounce" when walked on — you will want to investigate the cause carefully. The problem may be a basic structural one; the inability of the floor to support live weight loads.

WALLS

In the most fundamental sense, walls connect the floor and the roof and support the next floor system or roof. When walls have openings, like windows and/or doors, additional support is needed to carry the weight load. The extra support over such openings is called a header. Problems can develop at those locations if the header is not supporting the weight imposed. This problem would be particularly noticeable over a large opening, like a garage door. The solution is to increase the size of the header or add extra support to it. Neither is a simple job.

Walls should be checked to confirm they are plumb; i.e., vertically level. If the wall is out of plumb, it could indicate a settlement problem (which also would show up in the foundation). Or it could point to a structural problem caused by a roof system that is not properly braced, a condition which could cause the walls to bow out.

More often than not, when a wall is out of plumb it is that way because it was built that way. The Home Buyer's Warranty includes this construction standard:

"The walls should not be more than 1/2 inch out of plumb for any 8 foot vertical measurement."

Other wall topics (sheetrock, paint, wallpaper, etc.) are covered in Chapters Five and Six.

STAIRS

Although stairs and steps will be referred to here as though the words were synonymous, stairs actually are a flight of steps. A story — maybe apocryphal but probably true — popular among builders has to do with an elegant hotel in a major city that was built with a revolving restaurant "floating" atop the building. After construction was completed, the hotel owners learned to their dismay that the elevators would not accommodate the large commercial kitchen appliances purchased for the restaurant. And there was no other way to move them up. That intended gourmet restaurant is now, primarily, a popular cocktail lounge. Why that story here? When you are inspecting houses, make sure the stairwells will accept the furniture you plan to move in.

In a stairway, the height of each step (the rise) should be the same, and the width of each step (the tread) should not only be the same but should be deep enough to accommodate a large foot comfortably. Each step should be level, front to back and side to side. There should not be any bounce when weight is applied to each step. It is unusual to find any problems with steps. For safety reasons, any that are found should be corrected. Stairs and steps are major causes of accidents in the home. They should be constructed properly and safe, particularly if you have an elderly person or very young children in the family. Correction of a problem might be as simple as a little renailing to complete reconstruction.

CEILING

Ceilings are designed to be flat, vaulted (cathedral), trayed (graduated heights), domed . . . almost any configuration the architect and builder agree is feasible. Ceiling finishes can be paint, stippled, or otherwise textured. Sometimes beams are added as a decorative touch. Ceilings can be built to provide no attic storage, limited storage, or maximum storage. If maximum storage is to be provided, the ceiling must be constructed as another floor to accommodate the weight loads.

If an attic is used for storage but was not constructed for that purpose, you may find sagging in the ceiling. A builder generally will build the ceiling according to the planned use of the attic space. If you can stand in the attic, the builder probably has provided lumber in the ceiling adequate to support the attic weight load.

ROOF

The weight of the roof is distributed from the roof through the walls, then through the floor system to the foundation, then to the ground. Actually the walls support the roof and the roof steadies the walls. The roof system is braced off the walls for support.

Roofs typically are built in one of two ways: "stick built" — piece by piece construction on the home site; and with trusses, preassembled roof components. Trusses, which span from one outside wall to another, are installed on top of the walls one at a time, then braced against each other. Once the roof system is in place, the decking — the wood that covers the wood frame — is applied. A layer of felt paper follows, then the roofing shingles are nailed in place. Chapter Five includes more specific information on roofing shingles.

Roofs have different pitches or degrees of steepness. The pitch has more than one purpose. The design will give the house the desired look, but the degree of pitch will dictate the headroom available in the attic and the weight load bearing characteristics.

When you scrutinize a roof, look for an even appearance. If there is sagging between rafters, it could mean the proper decking was not used (perhaps the incorrect thickness). Correction requires replacement or addition of decking. If an entire section of the roof sags, spanning several rafters, it indicates that the wrong size rafters were used. This situation can be corrected by additional support or bracing of the rafters.

Next, look across the top of the roof. If the roof line is uneven, sagging in the middle, it may indicate a condition that could push the walls out. That sagging could be caused by improper bracing of the roof, generally poor construction work, or sometimes by settlement of an inside pier. The appearance of a bubble in the roof could be the result of the decking coming apart, or delaminating. In this case, the correction would be repairing or replacing the decking. Sometimes the decking merely needs to be renailed; it may be bowing because that simple step was not executed properly.

If the roof exterior does indicate a problem, inspection from inside the attic is appropriate. A truss roof is indistinguishable from a stick built roof from the outside. When you examine the underpart of the roof you can tell whether the lumber is sagging from the weight load or if any boards are bowing from the strain. If it looks as though the roof has an obvious problem, you would be well advised to seek professional advice. Corrections could be very costly.

WOOD TYPES & GRADES
The wood from which a house is constructed becomes part of the environment around it. If the moisture content of the air is higher than the moisture content of the wood, the wood will absorb moisture. As the moisture in the air is released, so the moisture in the wood will release also. A house actually "breathes". Wood is constantly moving to some degree as it expands and contracts while it absorbs and releases moisture.

Over a period of time, wood that is exposed to excess moisture will begin to conform to the weight loads imposed and will "forget" its original shape. A floor with a sag or bow will not return to what it was. It's new shape, or curve, has become its permanent shape. A sag in a floor or ceiling similarly is there to stay. Correction usually is replacement of the warped boards. Sometime this is an expensive and complicated correction.

It is obvious that all homes are not built the same; less obvious are the reasons why. Houses can be built with varying types and grades of wood. Once you have inspected a few houses, you will have come to understand that not all houses are built level, plumb, and square. In other words, appearances can be deceiving , not everything is what it appears to be, and some houses are better than others.

Some of the simplest things are not what they seem. A 2 x 4 is not a 2 x 4, it is a 1 1/2 x 3 1/2. This classic piece of wood, the backbone of construction lumber, used to be a true 2 x 4 . . . until planing to smooth it reduced it to its present (and universally accepted) size.

If you have two pieces of lumber of the same dimensions, you might have two different pieces of wood with very different strength characteristics. Not only are there hardwoods and softwoods, there are imported woods. Each has specific characteristics. Even two pieces of the same kind of wood will have differences within those specific characteristics because even the same wood will have grains that may differ piece by piece.

Grains are wide, medium, and dense. Even within the same type and grade, a dense grain will support more weight load than a wide grain. In addition, there are different grades of wood within the same family; e.g., Grade Mark #2 Yellow Pine and Grade Mark #3 Yellow Pine. One widely adopted grading system uses these terms: Select Structural #1, #2, #3 and construction, standard, utility. Each grade is able to support a different weight under identical conditions. Grade #1, for example, will support more than Grade #2 of the same type lumber. All lumber must be compared within exact categories to be accurate.

All lumber carries either an agency stamp or a mill stamp. Special agencies issue stamps to certain mills, certifying that the lumber is graded by the American Lumber Standards Committee standards. The A.L.S.C. follows procedures that were set up by the U.S. Department of Commerce. The stamp will indicate the type, grade, mill, and moisture content, but not necessarily the density (unless required). A mill stamp which adheres only to the issuing mill's standards usually shows the type and grade. Stamps from an agency and a mill may not represent the same quality lumber.

Some lumber is pressure treated; that is, given a preservative treatment to protect the wood. All pressure treated lumber is not the same either; quality ultimately depends on the type and grade lumber used and the quality/amount of chemical preservative applied.

Plywood is another lumber product available in varying qualities and thicknesses, and different numbers of layers within the same thickness. For example, 1/2 inch plywood comes with three or four layers, with four layers providing greater strength. Plywood is available for both interior and exterior use and is made from different types of wood with varying strength characteristics.

The information provided above on grades, types, and strengths of woods may exceed the "need to know" of the average buyer of residential property. If you are watching your house being built, plan to have a new house built, or may want to remodel an older house you are considering, it could be useful information.

Checklist #2: Basic Structural Elements, Foundation, and Framing

	House #1 Location:_____	NO PROBLEM	MINIMUM	MINOR	MAJOR	HOLD
		0	1	2	3	?
1	Does the foundation wall have vertical cracks?					
2	Is the vertical crack largest at the top? (costly repairs)					
3	Is the foundation structurally sound?					
4	Is the concrete workmanship acceptable?					
5	Are there expansion or settlement cracks in the concrete?					
6	Can you sweep up residue from the concrete repeatedly?					
7	Are there cracks in the driveway?					
8	Has the driveway been poorly resurfaced?					
9	Does the ground show thru anywhere in the driveway?					
10	Do you see any foundation cracks from the crawl space?					
11	Is there any wood replacement visible from the crawl space?					
12	Do you see any new or cracked piers in the crawl space?					
13	Do you see obvious alteration in pipes or ducts in the crawl space?					
14	If the house is on a slab can you see any cracks in the slab?					
15	Is there a musty smell inside the house (on a slab)?					
16	Does the slab floor feel damp?					
17	Will the exposed slab be used for additions? Level? Cracks?					
18	Do you see obvious curves in the basement walls?					
19	Are the basement walls damp?					
20	Does the basement have any leaks?					
21	What is the overall condition of any retainer walls?					
22	Are the floors level?					
23	Will any flooring need replacement?					
24	Are there excessive vibrations when you walk across the floors?					
25	Does the house have foundation and floor problems? (important)					
26	Is there any sagging over window and door openings?					
27	Are there any problems with stairs or steps?					
28	Does the ceiling sag?					
29	Will the roof require repair?					
30						
	SUB-TOTAL					

TRANSFER SUB-TOTALS TO
MASTER CHECKLIST FORM

ADDITIONAL REMARKS OR OTHERS:

_____

_____

_____

_____

_____

_____

_____

_____

_____

_____

_____

_____

_____

_____

Checklist #2: Basic Structural Elements, Foundation, and Framing

House #2

Location:_____

		NO PROBLEM	MINIMUM	MINOR	MAJOR	HOLD
		0	1	2	3	?
1	Does the foundation wall have vertical cracks?					
2	Is the vertical crack largest at the top? (costly repairs)					
3	Is the foundation structurally sound?					
4	Is the concrete workmanship acceptable?					
5	Are there expansion or settlement cracks in the concrete?					
6	Can you sweep up residue from the concrete repeatedly?					
7	Are there cracks in the driveway?					
8	Has the driveway been poorly resurfaced?					
9	Does the ground show thru anywhere in the driveway?					
10	Do you see any foundation cracks from the crawl space?					
11	Is there any wood replacement visible from the crawl space?					
12	Do you see any new or cracked piers in the crawl space?					
13	Do you see obvious alteration in pipes or ducts in the crawl space?					
14	If the house is on a slab can you see any cracks in the slab?					
15	Is there a musty smell inside the house (on a slab)?					
16	Does the slab floor feel damp?					
17	Will the exposed slab be used for additions? Level? Cracks?					
18	Do you see obvious curves in the basement walls?					
19	Are the basement walls damp?					
20	Does the basement have any leaks?					
21	What is the overall condition of any retainer walls?					
22	Are the floors level?					
23	Will any flooring need replacement?					
24	Are there excessive vibrations when you walk across the floors?					
25	Does the house have foundation and floor problems? (important)					
26	Is there any sagging over window and door openings?					
27	Are there any problems with stairs or steps?					
28	Does the ceiling sag?					
29	Will the roof require repair?					
30						
	SUB-TOTAL					

TRANSFER SUB-TOTALS TO
MASTER CHECKLIST FORM

ADDITIONAL REMARKS OR OTHERS: _____

_____

_____

_____

_____

_____

_____

_____

_____

_____

_____

_____

_____

_____

_____

_____

_____

Checklist #2: Basic Structural Elements, Foundation, and Framing

	House #3 Location:_____	NO PROBLEM	MINIMUM	MINOR	MAJOR	HOLD
		0	1	2	3	?
1	Does the foundation wall have vertical cracks?					
2	Is the vertical crack largest at the top? (costly repairs)					
3	Is the foundation structurally sound?					
4	Is the concrete workmanship acceptable?					
5	Are there expansion or settlement cracks in the concrete?					
6	Can you sweep up residue from the concrete repeatedly?					
7	Are there cracks in the driveway?					
8	Has the driveway been poorly resurfaced?					
9	Does the ground show thru anywhere in the driveway?					
10	Do you see any foundation cracks from the crawl space?					
11	Is there any wood replacement visible from the crawl space?					
12	Do you see any new or cracked piers in the crawl space?					
13	Do you see obvious alteration in pipes or ducts in the crawl space?					
14	If the house is on a slab can you see any cracks in the slab?					
15	Is there a musty smell inside the house (on a slab)?					
16	Does the slab floor feel damp?					
17	Will the exposed slab be used for additions? Level? Cracks?					
18	Do you see obvious curves in the basement walls?					
19	Are the basement walls damp?					
20	Does the basement have any leaks?					
21	What is the overall condition of any retainer walls?					
22	Are the floors level?					
23	Will any flooring need replacement?					
24	Are there excessive vibrations when you walk across the floors?					
25	Does the house have foundation and floor problems? (important)					
26	Is there any sagging over window and door openings?					
27	Are there any problems with stairs or steps?					
28	Does the ceiling sag?					
29	Will the roof require repair?					
30						

TRANSFER SUB-TOTALS TO
MASTER CHECKLIST FORM

| SUB-TOTAL | | | | |

ADDITIONAL REMARKS OR OTHERS:

3: Doors, Windows, and Exterior Finish

Once the frame of the house is completed you can begin to see the personality of the house come to life as the items that the trade calls "trim" are applied. Chapter three focuses exclusively on external trim; more specifically, such trim items as windows, doors, siding, porches, decks, and gutters. Variations of these items are also discussed. Basically we are considering what is visible from the outside of the house after the frame is in place.

DOORS AND WINDOWS

If doors and windows are to operate properly they must be installed level (horizontally straight) and plumb (vertically straight). Doors that are installed properly have equal margins or spaces between the door and the frame, at the top and sides. If they have been installed correctly, windows will open and close without difficulty. Many functional problems concerning windows and doors are caused by poor installation.

DOORS

When you examine the doors and door frames in a house, you expect to see that each door has equal margins. If the margin is not equal across the top, the door is out of level or out of plumb. In either case the door is not likely to be operating smoothly and should be reinstalled. When the margin is not the same on one side or the other, the door is out of plumb and re-hanging may be required.

After you have checked the margins, open and close the doors to see if the doors fit tightly against the frames when the doors are closed. If a door is particularly tight in one spot then it may be warped or out of level. Warped doors may require replacement. The *Home Buyer's Warranty* statement on warped doors is as follows:

"Exterior doors will warp to some degree due to temperature differential on inside and outside faces. However, they should not warp to the extent that they become inoperable or cease to be weather resistant or exceed National Woodwork Manufacturers Association Standards (1/4-inch).

Interior doors (full opening) should not warp to exceed National Woodwork Manufacturers Association Standards (1/4-inch), provided the proper levels of humidity have been maintained in the home."

When the door is still closed check to see if you can move the door back and forth with the handle. A door should fit snugly within the door frame. If a closed door is loose, it's likely the lock needs adjusting. Do the hinges squeak when you open the door? The cause for the squeak could be something simple (like the door hinges needing oil) or something expensive, like a warped door placing strain on the frame.

Door locks sometimes become hard to open and door handles work loose. The lock may be in need of replacement, or it may merely need to be oiled or tightened. Door locks and hinges require normal maintenance. If a lock is broken and needs to be replaced you may have difficulty finding an exact duplicate, but chances are you will be able to locate a suitable replacement.

Exterior doors usually are keyed alike; i.e., the same key will open any door. When you need to replace an exterior lock you probably can have the new lock keyed to match the old one, either by a locksmith or at the store where the new lock was purchased. Our local expert (Pat Northrop of Gaddy Lumber in metropolitan Atlanta) says that if the old key will fit into the new lock, it generally can be keyed to match.

TYPES OF DOORS

Doors are doors. It is the composition that makes one different from another. Doors are made of solid wood, hollow core or solid laminated wood products, and insulated metal or are metal formed. Bifold doors are made from wood or metal, as are louvered doors. Sliding doors (where one side slides behind another) and pocket doors (where the door slides into the wall) are spacesavers, because they do not use the area that a door normally uses to open.

Usually, all the interior doors in a house are identical. Hollow core laminated doors are made of two pieces of wood, or Masonite, which is pressed together against a frame. The most common problem with hollow core doors is punch

holes. The door bumper, which stops the door from hitting the wall behind it, has a tendency over time to penetrate the hollow part of the door, making an unsightly hole. Patching usually fills the hole without totally concealing it. The good news about hollow core doors is that they are relatively inexpensive.

You will probably find hollow core doors in the best of new houses because they are acceptable substitutes for expensive solid wood interior doors. The materials used to make the hollow core door are compressed and molded to give them an appearance similar to the six panel solid wood doors. Hollow core laminated doors do not shrink and crack in the ways a solid wood door might. When you are making house-to-house value comparisons, consider the type, style and number of doors in the house — but don't necessarily be "turned off" by hollow core doors.

Exterior doors should fit snugly against the floor and door frame to prevent drafts or water from entering. Front doors come in a wide variety of styles; single or double doors, plain glass inserts to stained glass inserts, with or without side lights (glass on the sides), and with or without insulation. Wood exterior doors are better suited for locations under porches, where exposure to water and excessive moisture is kept to a minimum. Proper maintenance is very important for exterior wood doors because it protects them from moisture absorption; that can be the beginning of wood rot and the kind of swelling that affects the door's ability to function.

Sliding glass doors (accessing a patio, for example) have tracks that need to be checked for wear. An older sliding glass door may need to have its track replaced. All sliding glass doors should be made of safety or tempered glass. In fact, most building codes now require that.

Safety glass will not shatter into dangerous jagged pieces because of the plastic film laminated between two pieces of glass.

WINDOWS

The easiest and most effective way to examine windows is to open and close them. Do they operate properly? Check the space at the bottom of the window just before it is closed. Is this space even from left to right? If the space is not equal the window may be out of plumb. An out of plumb window will bind when you attempt to open or close it. The window will need to be re-installed if it is to function correctly.

Balances are the weights or springs on each side of a window that allow the window to be opened without much effort and hold the window in place after opening. If the balances are not adjusted equally or if one balance is not working properly, the window will be difficult to open. If a window that has been opened will not stay open it's likely a balance is broken. If problems with balances are not corrected, you will continue to have a problem with that window, and you probably will experience deterioration of other window parts as well. The correction is prompt adjustment or replacement of the balances.

You will also want to check the locks on the windows. Broken or badly worn locks should be replaced. Certainly the locks that are used the most are the ones that will wear out first. However, locks that have force placed on them in the wrong areas also will wear out quickly. A broken lock can mean that the window is installed poorly. The resulting stress places the lock in a bind. As you should in virtually every area of home inspection, try to look "beneath the surface" to understand the real scope of any problem. In this case, the (relatively inexpensive) lock problem may be a more expensive window problem.

When a pane in a window is broken, a glass shop can replace it quite easily. Broken windows certainly should be replaced, as should be any window panes that are cracked. Rain and moisture will seep through and cause damage. Any necessary window repairs should be on the seller's "Things to Repair" list.

When you are checking the windows for breakage or other damage, you also should inspect the screens (and the storm windows, if the house is in a temperature zone that requires them). The screens should be in good condition and fit against the outside window frame securely. Finally, before leaving the windows, look for evidence of any water stains or damage around the windows, especially at the sills, which may indicate the presence of a leak.

Like houses, windows are available in different shapes and sizes, are constructed in a variety of ways, and are available at costs ranging from very low to exceedingly high. When you are making your house-to-house value comparisons, try to understand and consider the kinds and value of windows in each. Also, appreciate the fact that while more windows usually improve the design/appearance of a house, they represent more heat loss and higher heating bills.

TYPES OF WINDOWS

Basically, there are two kinds of window construction: wood frame and metal frame. The geometric design of the window is the factor that makes one window appear different from another. Windows are identified by the number of panes in each window. They are either single hung or double hung (a single hung window has only one part that moves, the double hung has two). In some cases a window will have more than two moving parts; an example — the jalousie windows used extensively in Florida and elsewhere. A fixed glass, or stationary, window does not open. A window that has six panes over another six panes is called a six over six or a twelve light. If just one panel of six moves, it is called a six over six, single hung.

Metal windows are made of different gauges (thicknesses) of metal. The window glass itself also comes in different thicknesses. Metal frames are available in different colors, like bronze and almond. Today, in houses in the medium to low price range, metal windows are being used extensively because of their lower cost and easier maintenance.

INSULATED WINDOWS AND DOORS

Windows have interior and exterior sides and are built to satisfy both inside and outside criteria, but doors are built for interior or exterior use only. The degree to which a window or exterior door insulates is important, for both home comfort and energy cost control. There are many fine insulated products on the market today. All have an "R Factor" rating. The higher the rating, the better the insulating ability.

Insulated doors are metal cased and filled with some type of insulating material. They have either magnetic or fiber weatherstripping, which helps seal the door and prevent drafts. Insulated doors come in many styles, and they don't crack, rot or swell.

Insulated windows have double panes; two pieces of glass, with an air space, sealed together to prevent condensation between the glass. A similar kind of glass/air/glass insulation can be obtained with the use of storm windows. The effectiveness of the insulation will depend upon the fit and the air space between the two windows. Something else to bear in mind; while more, rather than fewer, windows and doors enhance the appearance of most houses, the more there are — the more square footage the house has in window and door space — the more energy will be used to heat and cool the house.

If this choice is consistent with your overall house selection, choose insulated windows and doors. They will give you lower energy costs year after year. Consider them as an investment, because they give you a return in the form of lower heating/cooling bills.

GARAGE DOORS

The standard single garage door is 7 feet high by 8 feet wide; the standard double door 16 feet wide. You will need to know the garage will accommodate your car(s) comfortably. Like any other door, garage doors need to fit tightly against the frame and they should open and close without problems.

If the door feels overly heavy when you open or close it, or is just difficult to open, the cause could be a problem with the door hardware. The door should open without twisting or binding in the tracks. Balances apply a certain amount of tension on the doors and they may not be adjusted properly. A warped door will also bind or it may try to jump the track. It's also possible that poor installation has put the door "out of square", causing it to bind. The hardware, including the locks, should be checked for wear. If the garage door is equipped with an automatic opener, test it with your car to ensure it is in working order.

OUTSIDE FINISH: SIDING AND CORNICE

Siding and cornice are the exterior finishes. Siding is simple to define because it is the product that covers the sides of the house. The definition of cornice sounds a little complicated. Cornice is the covering, usually wood, applied to the overhang of the roof. Cornice has two parts; the soffit, a piece of wood that runs perpendicular to the side of the house and is under the roof overhang and the fascia board, which is parallel to the siding and the part of the cornice to which the gutters are attached. The fascia "faces" out and the soffit is hardly seen — unless you stand under the roof overhang and look up.

Cornices usually are wood or aluminum, but siding is made from many different products. It can be brick, rock, stucco, wood, masonite, aluminum, or vinyl. Siding is placed over sheathing, which is applied to a house before the siding (brick, wood, stucco, etc.) is applied. (The differences in sheathing is discussed in chapter five under insulation).

If you know what to look for, the outside appearance can tell you about the condition of the house. You need to look closely at the cornice, gutters, garage doors, and siding. You may find that a freshly puttied and repainted house (that looks great from the street) is concealing an advanced case of wood rot. Wood rot can be patched and painted, and it will look nice to the casual inspector. But look closely for numerous putty marks. Putty covered with paint has a shinier texture. Chances are that a house that has rotten wood covered up with putty and paint also will have other problems that are disguised.

Look closely for any water stains on the soffit or siding that indicate water penetrating behind the wood, causing damage (wood rot). Wood rot is more likely to occur where wood is not protected by paint, water enters because of a leak, and at places where water is trapped against the wood.

Metal flashing is used over some windows and doors that do not have sufficient roof overhang or are not protected by a porch. The flashing keeps water from entering at these points. Wood or metal drip cap is used to keep water out where siding meets brick, rock, or stucco or two different siding meet on a horizontal plane. Where metal flashing is in place, you should examine it for rust or corrosion. If it is damaged it will need to be replaced.

While flashing plays an important part in the prevention of water damage, caulking is equally important. Caulking is a sealant, applied with a caulking gun at precise points on the house to protect it from the elements. It should always be applied where the siding meets windows, doors, or the corner boards of the house. "Corner boards" are the exterior vertical boards at the corners of a house. If caulking has not been done, or has not been properly maintained, you can anticipate the wood damage and the eventual need for replacement. When you check the siding, also check the decorative trim items to be sure they are in good condition and properly secured.

BRICK

Typically, when someone speaks of a brick house that person usually has a mental image of a house that has all sides covered with brick. Today, in an economizing market, you may find that even the more expensive houses have a brick front (face), and the remainder of the house is sided with wood or other material. When comparing houses you will want to remember the maintenance advantages of a fully bricked house over a partially bricked house with wood siding. The wood siding, of course, will require periodic painting. Some house advertisements describe bricked front houses as "brick"; you do not learn the truth until you actually see the house.

Bricks are available in a variety of sizes and colors. They are produced in batches of tens of thousands, and no two batches (even produced to the same specification) are exactly the same color. Some brick styles, with names like Plantation, Classic Red, and Salem, have been made for many years. The best feature of brick is the low/no maintenance factor. Although you might think it would be, it is not as good an insulator as wood.

If you wanted to add to a brick house, you would come closest to matching the original brick if it were one of the traditional brick styles. A room addition to a brick house probably would not match exactly, but you could use an architectural diversion to offset the slight color variation. Unfortunately, the same type brick may not be available at all. Painting or stuccoing all the brick and creating a completely new look is an alternative.

Brick are supported by the foundation. Brick "ties" are placed in the foundation wall and nailed periodically to studs of the frame. As the bricks are put in place the ties are laid in the mortar between the bricks. Brick ties help hold the brick in place straight and tight against the house.

A proper brick job should have the same width mortar joints (the bond between the bricks). The brick should be level and the walls should be plumb. At the point where the brick meets the top of the house you should be able to see a level margin and gauge the levelness of the brick. If you find that this line is not straight, you know that the brick or the cornice is out of level. This unevenness is a cosmetic problem, not structural, so there would be no correction.

While you are observing the mortar joints you need to check the consistency of the mortar at several different locations. Use a stick to gently scrape the joint. A brick mortar joint should not be sandy or powdery and you should not be able to penetrate it with your stick. If you can, you know that the mortar mix is not good at that site.

Brick mortar is mixed in relatively small batches and applied by hand with a trowel. Every house, therefore, will have multiple batches of mortar. A poor mix could have had too much sand added to it. You probably will be able to spot a poorly mixed area, because too much sand changes the shade of the mortar. Freezing before it dries completely is another reason for bad mortar. It's unlikely, because of the many batches mixed and used, that all the mortar will be bad. However, you should replace the bad mortar. The weather will continue to wash it out and you could possibly have brick coming loose.

When you examine a brick house you need to look for cracks or bows in the brick walls. If you recall (from the information on stress and settlement cracks in the chapter on foundations), any stress cracks in the bricks will also be vertical in nature. Stress cracks in brick may or may not follow the brick joints. Settlement cracks normally follow the course of least resistance which means that they zig-zag at any angle that is easiest. In a severe case a stress crack can break the bricks apart as it continues up or down the wall. Seek professional advice quickly if you come across this unusual situation. The correction would be both extensive and expensive. Multiple stress cracks following the joints also should be avoided, as these are evidence of structural defects. Hairline cracks (non-structural and horizontal) in the mortar joints are only normal expansion cracks.

The size and width of either expansion or stress cracks are what you need to consider. The Home Buyer's Warranty Program standard states that:

"Small cracks are common in mortar joints of masonry construction. Cracks greater than 1/8 inch in width are considered excessive."

A bow in a brick wall may mean that the bricks are pulling away from the house. It can also mean that the brick tie spacing was not proper or that ties were not used at all. A footing that is not the proper size can be another cause for a bow in a brick wall. The footing gives away and the brick pulls away from the house. Poor construction may be the only cause for a bow in a brick wall, particularly if there is no other evidence to point towards a primary cause; e.g., cracks in the brick and foundation. If the bricks are pulling away from the house, the correction must follow the cause. Basically that means starting over: the brick must come down; a cracked foundation must be repaired; a footing must be reinforced; brick ties must be added; etc.

As you are checking for bows and cracks, you can examine the cornice at the point that it meets the brick. "Eyeball" this area as you look down the house, to see if the wall is level. A wavy, in and out, pattern at this point means that the brick is out of plumb. It's likely it was built out of plumb. Fortunately, this is an aesthetic distraction, not a structural problem — but it could be an expensive problem. Correction for an out of plumb condition usually is not feasible because it involves starting over.

Generally you will find that a brick house is constructed correctly, with perhaps a slight, non-structural variation here or there. Structural cracks through the brick and foundation probably are the only condition that would discourage your purchase of the property. Brick's low maintenance cost definitely is a major factor to consider when you review and compare the maintenance budget of different houses.

ROCK

Rock and stone are man's oldest building materials. In this chapter rock and stone are referred to interchangeably. Although rock and stone are bulky and thick, neither insulates as well as wood. On the other hand, wood does decay. Also bear in mind that rock and stone don't need a coat of paint every five years or so. Clearly, each siding material has its own advantages.

Rock is applied in two basic ways. In the first way the rock is stacked upon and supported by the foundation in much the same way as brick. Rock also can be held in place by metal lath (wire mesh). The size of the rock determines the method of installation that is used. Thicker rock is stacked upon the foundation and held in place with brick ties; thin rock put in place with metal lath.

Metal lath is a wire mesh that is nailed or fastened to the outside walls of the house. Next, a mortar mix is put into the lath and allowed to dry, forming a base structure. The rock are then set in place one at a time, using mortar on the back as an adhesive. After the mortar has dried and the rocks are set in place, the spaces between the rocks are filled with mortar.

Mortar joints may fall from around the rock. This would happen if the mortar was not pressed into the spaces. Since the metal lath is the supporting factor it must be secured to the wall correctly. If this is not done, the weight of the rock may pull the metal lathing away from the house, causing the rock wall to bow. In a "worst case" scenario, the rock siding could fall away completely.

Since rocks do not normally crack, you are not apt to see a crack running through a rock wall. Stress or settlement cracks in rock follow the mortar joints. When metal lath is used some hairline expansion cracks are normal. You should check the rock wall for stress cracks above and below the rock because the crack may be behind the rock.

STUCCO

Traditional stucco is a mortar mixture finish that is applied to the exterior of a house. A true stucco finish is a classic style that has been used on famous homes and estates around the world. Recently, the construction marketplace has seen an proliferation of pseudo-stucco products. These products have acrylic bonding ingredients. Acrylics have good qualities, like fast drying and easy application. Should you choose to buy a stucco-finished house, you will want to investigate the type of stucco that has been applied.

Stucco usually is applied in one of three different ways. Many times a thin layer of stucco mixture is applied over bare block to enhance the appearance. This is a cosmetic application and is not intended to be anything more. When a house has an exposed concrete block foundation, most builders will stucco the exposed area. Any hairline cracks in this stucco "topcoat" would be superficial, but don't mistake cracks that go through to the block. These could be structural.

The classic application of stucco (and the most common) is done with metal lath and is similar to rock application. A mortar and/or concrete mix is troweled into the wire mesh. Usually two coats make up the base and then a third finishing coat is applied with the desired pattern and color. After the third stucco application a sealant or paint is applied. If expansion joints were not put in place, the third application may have hairline expansion cracks. This type application can also have curing cracks if it dries too quickly. Curing cracks look like extremely fine eggshell cracks but they are only superficial. A coat of paint would cover them.

The metal lath can loosen and cause the stucco wall to bow. The wall might also bow if the primary wall was not built straight. Moisture can penetrate between the stucco layers, causing them to pop away from the wall. Each of these problems would require redoing of the stucco wall, sometimes all the way down to the frame.

The intent of this book is to make you a knowledgeable inspector and evaluator of all kinds of residential properties, every possible structural condition. As in every section, the information presented is intended to be informative (never implicitly negative) about a particular kind of structure, material, finish, etc. That certainly is true of the analysis presented here regarding stucco. Generally speaking, a properly constructed stucco house is a very attractive, low maintenance home.

The third way stucco is applied is with the use of a fiber mesh sheathing that is applied to the exterior sheathing. A thin mix of cement and synthetic material is then applied, followed by a finish coat that creates the pattern and color desired. A number of problems may arise from the use of this kind of application: the primary sheathing could separate from the house; the fiber mesh may come loose from the sheathing; bubbles could develop in the stucco, indicating that the mesh is loose; or stucco popping off the wall may indicate that moisture entered the surface because it was not sealed properly.

Stucco surfaces that don't have waterproofing in the mix need to be sealed to prevent moisture from entering and freezing. Hairline expansion cracks are not a problem because the synthetic material is intended to expand and contract. Any stress or settlement cracks in this stucco are a problem of the primary wall. These conditions call for your thorough investigation.

You should check all stucco surfaces for patches regardless of the kind of application used; the pattern or color of an area that has been patched may be slightly off, not quite matching its surroundings. Patches obviously indicate that something has happened. It is important for you to know what caused the need for the patch; it may not have cured the situation, merely covered it up.

WOOD

Wood is the most popular siding material. There are many different widths, thicknesses, and types of wood sidings, virtually all of which are available unfinished, primed, or finished. You can get different thicknesses in the same type siding. A thick siding is stronger and it helps hold the frame of the house in alignment. It also has the ability to disguise the normal ups and downs of the crowns in the wood that was used in the frame. A thin siding, unable to provide this quality, has a wavy appearance. There are grade variances in wood siding as there are in other lumber products. Some siding expands and contracts more than others because of differences in the wood.

Most siding is lapped, either horizontally or vertically, one piece overlapping the other. Different sidings require different lap applications. Of course, the more overlap, the more siding is needed to cover the house. The laps in the siding, like mortar joints on brickwork, should be the same width. You can use the cornice to judge the levelness of the siding. If you see that the distances between the boards are inconsistent, one or the other — the cornice or the siding — is out of level. Sometimes the lap is lessened (say, from one inch to one-half inch) in an effort to "cut corners". This may result in exposure of the insulating sheathing underneath when the siding contracts, as a natural response to the environment. You will want to check the lap points to see that no sheathing shows from underneath. Incorrectly lapped siding needs to be re-applied; otherwise, over a period of time, rain or moisture will enter

at the openings and the siding would begin to deteriorate. If this problem were allowed to continue it could develop into wood rot of the mainframe. Incorrectly lapped siding should be redone. You will be able to salvage most of the old siding if care is taken when it is removed.

All siding is not attached to the house in the same way. Siding nails should be nailed through the siding and into a supporting board of the frame. Both overnailing or undernailing present problems. When the siding is overnailed, the wood splits or cracks. When it is undernailed the boards warp for lack of support.

Wood needs room to expand and contract. All nails used in siding need to be rustproof. If the correct nails are not used, the nails will rust, and leaving unsightly streaks down the siding. The only correction is to replace the nails. Repainting will conceal the rust only temporarily,;in time, it will bleed through. All wood siding splits to some extent, but an excessive amount of split siding usually indicates an improper nail job. Split siding needs to be replaced with new siding.

Stress or settlement cracks will not normally crack wood siding but they will pull or move the siding away from the house. If one section of the house has splits and cracks in the siding, it probably is evidence that there is a structural problem there. A problem isolated to one area of the house is not normal, and the cause for it should be investigated. You may find that the carpenter's helper was nailing in that area. Remember that no structural problem exists in a vacuum; there is always a corroborating cause. It is not always visible, but it often is basic to the structural integrity of the house.

HARDBOARD (Masonite)

Masonite is one of those almost-generic terms

with which almost everyone is familiar. Actually Masonite is a trade name for a pressed hardboard siding product. Hardboard siding is applied in the same manner as wood siding. It is made in different widths and with different finishes and is usually primed with a basecoat. Some types have an embossing that resembles woodgrain, others have very smooth finishes.

Hardboard siding comes in two grades. Grade A is first quality, Grade B refers to second quality irregulars with some imperfection(s). If the siding is flaking or pulling apart, it probably is Grade B. All hardboard siding, Grade A and Grade B, is not the same. Depending upon its composition, the siding will expand and contract to varying degrees. Manufacturers of hardboard siding issue different lap requirements and nailing procedures. These must be followed to achieve the maximum results.

Hardboard siding normally will show more waves in the framed walls because it bends between the framing studs more than wood siding does. The composition of hardboard siding makes it very difficult to crack. This characteristic is the primary reason for its use. Still, you should examine this siding as thoroughly as you would wood siding. If the hardboard siding has cracked, the house has a serious problem; one that probably is stress related and structural in nature.

ALUMINUM / VINYL
Aluminum and vinyl sidings are manufactured in a variety of styles, patterns, colors, and thicknesses. In the case of either aluminum or vinyl, the thicker the material, the better the siding. Both these sidings are nailed loose and one piece interlocks to the next, covering the nails. The vinyl siding needs the space to expand and contract. Aluminum dents quite easily but vinyl does

not. Both vinyl and aluminum siding offer the advantage of minimum maintenance, a point in their favor.

New homes have these sidings applied over the sheathing, just like any other siding material. However, aluminum and vinyl also are primary residing materials, used over old siding to give houses a new look and/or to cut down on painting maintenance. One concern with a house that has been resided or double sided might be the justification for the new siding. You will want to ask why. New siding over rotten or damaged wood will not stop the wood from deteriorating if there is a moisture source still present. This deterioration could spread to the main frame. It is better to ask and be informed than to sign a contract without knowing, and find that you have inherited a significant problem.

PORCHES / DECKS
Neither porches or decks are intended to fulfill any structural function in a house. They are attractive, and can make a house more enjoyable. Often, one or both are added to a house to achieve a certain look more than for any other reason. The lumber used for both should be pressure treated or, at least, coated with waterproofing. The nails should be rustproof. Check to see if the porches or decks are level and that the supporting columns are plumb. Because these areas are exposed to the elements, you should look closely for rotten wood.

Is the deck or porch secure to the house? Does it shake or move when you walk across it? If so, it clearly is not safe. Do you see any bows or sags in the floor? They can develop when the proper size wood is not used for the spans. The railing and steps should also be secure and be strong enough to support a heavy weight load — for times like the 4th of July family barbecue. The pickets in the rail need to be close enough that small children can not fall through as they play.

GUTTERS

The gutters are applied to a house for the purpose of systematically carrying to the ground the rain-water that falls on the roof. Gutters are installed slightly out of level so the water will flow to the downspouts. Gutters are made of different materials, typically galvanized metal and aluminum. If aluminum is the material of choice, the gutters come in different sizes, thicknesses, and colors.

If gutters have not properly maintained (leaves and other debris cleaned out periodically), you may find they have been the cause behind water damage at the roof line. When water can not flow freely through the gutters and out the downspouts, it will overflow, with some of the water running back onto the cornice. This problem may also develop if the gutters are under-sized for the square footage of the roof. Check the cornice to see if it has any water stains on the soffit. Water stains may mean wood damage. Are the gutters and down spouts secure ? Do you see rust anywhere? This might indicate that the gutters need to be replaced. Paint flaking from the gutters of a newly painted house probably means that the gutters were not primed before the new coat of paint was applied.

Checklist #3: Doors, Windows, and Exterior Finish

	House #1 Location:_____	NO PROBLEM	MINIMUM	MINOR	MAJOR	HOLD
		0	1	2	3	?
1	Have all the doors been instaled properly?					
2	Will any doors require re-installation?					
3	Are there any warped doors requiring replacement?					
4	Do the door locks function correctly?					
5	Are the windows operating properly?					
6	Will any windows require part or total replacement?					
7	Are there any broken window locks?					
8	Does any window glass need replacing? Screens?					
9	Do the garage doors work properly?					
10	Does the house have any significant water stains? Wood rot?					
11	Is the caulking properly applied and/or maintained?					
12	Brick House: Is the mortar joint mix consistently good?					
13	Brick House: Do you see any bows in the walls?					
14	Brick House: Are there any stress or settlement cracks?					
15	Rock siding: Is any mortar falling away from the rock?					
16	Rock siding: Do you see any cracks in the rock wall?					
17	Stucco siding: Are there any bows in the walls?					
18	Stucco siding: Is any stucco popping loose?					
19	Stucco siding: Can you identify any problems with the fiber mesh?					
20	Stucco siding: Do you see any patches in the walls?					
21	Wood siding: Is there any exposed sheathing between the boards?					
22	Wood siding: Has the siding been nailed properly?					
23	Wood siding: Do you see any split siding? In an isolated area?					
24	Hardboard siding: Are any boards cracked?					
25	Aluminum/Vinyl siding: What was the reason for residing?					
26	Are the porches and decks safe and structurally sound?					
27	Are the gutters secure?					
28	Do you see any water damage at the roof line?					
29	REMARKS OR OTHER:					
30						

TRANSFER SUB-TOTALS TO
MASTER CHECKLIST FORM

SUB-TOTAL				

ADDITIONAL REMARKS OR OTHERS:

_____

_____

_____

_____

_____

_____

_____

_____

_____

_____

_____

_____

_____

_____

_____

_____

_____

Checklist #3: Doors, Windows, and Exterior Finish

House #2

Location:_____

		NO PROBLEM	MINIMUM	MINOR	MAJOR	HOLD
		0	1	2	3	?
1	Have all the doors been instaled properly?					
2	Will any doors require re-installation?					
3	Are there any warped doors requiring replacement?					
4	Do the door locks function correctly?					
5	Are the windows operating properly?					
6	Will any windows require part or total replacement?					
7	Are there any broken window locks?					
8	Does any window glass need replacing? Screens?					
9	Do the garage doors work properly?					
10	Does the house have any significant water stains? Wood rot?					
11	Is the caulking properly applied and/or maintained?					
12	Brick House: Is the mortar joint mix consistently good?					
13	Brick House: Do you see any bows in the walls?					
14	Brick House: Are there any stress or settlement cracks?					
15	Rock siding: Is any mortar falling away from the rock?					
16	Rock siding: Do you see any cracks in the rock wall?					
17	Stucco siding: Are there any bows in the walls?					
18	Stucco siding: Is any stucco popping loose?					
19	Stucco siding: Can you identify any problems with the fiber mesh?					
20	Stucco siding: Do you see any patches in the walls?					
21	Wood siding: Is there any exposed sheathing between the boards?					
22	Wood siding: Has the siding been nailed properly?					
23	Wood siding: Do you see any split siding? In an isolated area?					
24	Hardboard siding: Are any boards cracked?					
25	Aluminum/Vinyl siding: What was the reason for residing?					
26	Are the porches and decks safe and structurally sound?					
27	Are the gutters secure?					
28	Do you see any water damage at the roof line?					
29	REMARKS OR OTHER:					
30						

TRANSFER SUB-TOTALS TO
MASTER CHECKLIST FORM

SUB-TOTAL

ADDITIONAL REMARKS OR OTHERS:

Checklist #3: Doors, Windows, and Exterior Finish

	House #3 Location:_____	NO PROBLEM	MINIMUM	MINOR	MAJOR	HOLD
		0	1	2	3	?
1	Have all the doors been instaled properly?					
2	Will any doors require re-installation?					
3	Are there any warped doors requiring replacement?					
4	Do the door locks function correctly?					
5	Are the windows operating properly?					
6	Will any windows require part or total replacement?					
7	Are there any broken window locks?					
8	Does any window glass need replacing? Screens?					
9	Do the garage doors work properly?					
10	Does the house have any significant water stains? Wood rot?					
11	Is the caulking properly applied and/or maintained?					
12	Brick House: Is the mortar joint mix consistently good?					
13	Brick House: Do you see any bows in the walls?					
14	Brick House: Are there any stress or settlement cracks?					
15	Rock siding: Is any mortar falling away from the rock?					
16	Rock siding: Do you see any cracks in the rock wall?					
17	Stucco siding: Are there any bows in the walls?					
18	Stucco siding: Is any stucco popping loose?					
19	Stucco siding: Can you identify any problems with the fiber mesh?					
20	Stucco siding: Do you see any patches in the walls?					
21	Wood siding: Is there any exposed sheathing between the boards?					
22	Wood siding: Has the siding been nailed properly?					
23	Wood siding: Do you see any split siding? In an isolated area?					
24	Hardboard siding: Are any boards cracked?					
25	Aluminum/Vinyl siding: What was the reason for residing?					
26	Are the porches and decks safe and structurally sound?					
27	Are the gutters secure?					
28	Do you see any water damage at the roof line?					
29	REMARKS OR OTHER:					
30						
	SUB-TOTAL					

TRANSFER SUB-TOTALS TO
MASTER CHECKLIST FORM

ADDITIONAL REMARKS OR OTHERS:

4: Plumbing, Electrical, Heating, and Air Conditioning

This chapter covers such auxiliary items as plumbing, heating, cooling, electricity, and related equipment. There is an extremely wide quality range in the equipment, components, and materials used for these auxiliaries; greater differences than in any other area of the house. These product quality and performance differences may only be insignificant, or they can be extreme. How does anyone recognize and understand these differences? It isn't easy when most manufacturers call their products "the best", or the "top of the line."

Ratings established by impartial consumer testing groups can help, but they don't always provide complete answers, nor do they always test all the products available. You need to know what is best suited to your needs and to begin at that point to investigate those items that pertain to your household. Questions to ask yourself might include: Do I want gas or electric service in the kitchen? Do I want central air conditioning or will window units in the bedrooms be satisfactory? Since the real answer to what is best depends upon personal needs you will want to understand basic differences in the products you are evaluating in order to make the decisions that best satisfy those personal needs.

PLUMBING

When you consider the variables involved with the plumbing of a house you probably will be surprised at how many there are. First, you will want to know if the water system is public or private. If it is public, the county or city provides and maintains it. Private systems are totally independent of a municipal system. Two examples of private systems are well water and a septic system. It is not uncommon for a house to utilize a combination; perhaps public water and an individual septic system. Once you know the house both acquires and disposes of water, you can begin to look at the plumbing "hardware", the pipes, faucets, sinks, etc.

WELLS

In many parts of the country, wells are still a primary source of water. Wells usually are either bored or drilled. A bored well is about thirty inches in diameter and usually less than one hundred feet deep. A drilled well is deeper, usually at least one hundred and fifty feet, but the diameter is only approximately six inches. The drilled well system is more reliable because its depth offers a more pure and continuous water supply.

In either kind of well, the water pressure is determined by the pump's size and type. Both the bored well system and the drilled well system should be "closed" systems. In a closed system, the shaft is "cased" and the top is "capped." Nothing can get into the water system to contaminate it. However, not all wells are. Some older ones, especially, are not. Regardless of casing, all well water should be tested once a year — or anytime there is a change in the quality of the water (taste, color, odor, etc.).You also should test if the seal of the well has been broken.

The amount of water that a well will produce before running dry is certainly important. What determines the amount of water available to the user is the quantity of water in the ground and the time necessary to replenish it. You will want to know the amount of water that the well produces and the average refill time. It would be useful to compare the present size family to your own and determine a "use ratio." If a well is capable of producing eight hundred gallons per day this does not mean that all eight hundred gallons are available within a limited period. If the well has a more limited production capacity, families usually have to adapt to a time schedule in order to prevent the water supply from dropping too low. Baths and clothes washing may have to be scheduled at different times to allow for sufficient water.

A storage tank can be used in order to extend the life of a water pump. Storage tanks come in many sizes. They help to maintain pressure in the water line so the pump does not come on each time a faucet is used. One type of tank is a direct feed. When the water is turned on and the pressure is reduced, the pump comes on and pumps water into the tank. Then the water travels to the faucet. With this type tank, it is almost like having the pump hooked directly to the water pipe. An air pressurized storage tank works like a direct feed tank but with more pressure. There-

fore more water is available before the water pump comes on. A certain air pressure must be maintained in this tank; because the water absorbs some of the air, air must be added periodically. Another storage tank has a vinyl bag inside which separates the water from the air and in this way the air pressure is maintained.

Occasional cloudy or muddy water is not uncommon with wells. There are many causes for this condition, some serious, some not. When there has been heavy or prolonged rain a cracked or poorly joined casing can allow seepage of dirt into the well. If there is no casing on the well the same thing can happen. A well that is poorly capped can have seepage from the surface water. Cloudy or muddy water also can develop when the pick up point of the water is too close to the bottom of the well. When that happens, the normal sediment at the bottom is brought up along with the water. Filters can be added to take out impurities and sediment.

Increases and decreases in the water's Ph level can cause problems. The mineral content in water can give it a certain taste; e.g. some Florida water has a sulfurous taste. Your county extension agent or local health department will be a very good source for information concerning maintenance of and problems with wells. Don't be dismayed if the home you are looking at is served by well water. Usually a well is a good water source. In many cases the water quality is considerably better than the city water available in overpopulated urban areas.

SEPTIC TANKS

A septic tank is a large underground tank, part of a system designed to hold and dispose of waste (sewage). It has a system of drain lines that lead from the tank to allow the liquid portion of the waste to be absorbed and evaporated. Usually a house is either connected to a municipal sewerage system or it has a septic tank. The size of a septic tank is determined by the number of bedrooms in a house. The belief is that statistic will most accurately reflect the number of people using the septic tank. A second factor that influences the size of a tank, and whether a septic tank can be used at all, is the condition of the ground. In other words how well does the ground absorb water ? This ground absorption capability is called the "perk rate."

A septic tank can be pumped out when it is not functioning properly. You might want to ask the seller if the tank has ever been pumped out and if so, when? If there is room in the yard, additional lines can be added or existing lines can be lengthened to help the system work more efficiently. A gravel pit at the end of a line will increase the absorbency of a marginal system. Heavy or prolonged rain can influence the working of a septic tank by saturating the ground. A marginal tank might not work at all under these conditions.

When a septic tank is performing badly, the water drains very slowly or not at all. An example is the drainage of a tub located on the second floor. The septic tank blockage will begin to back up the drainpipes in the first story, then begin to effect the second story drainage. It is very important to ask about any drainage problems. If the septic system is not working efficiently, draining the tank does not solve the problem, and extension of the lines is not possible, you may have to consider tapping into municipal sewer lines. If sewer lines are not available, you would seem to have an insurmountable problem.

Another common problem that may interfere with septic tank efficiency is invasion by tree roots. As a tree grows so, of course, do the roots. These roots seek out water. The septic tank system provides an abundance of water so the tree roots grow into the lines and cause the system to malfunction. There are products on the market whose function it is to kill small tree roots. Unfortunately, they also kill the necessary bacteria that breaks down the waste matter in the tank. And the additive is only a temporary remedy anyway, because the roots keep growing. It is best to place the lines well away from trees in the first place.

There are also products that help the bacteria in the tank break down the waste. If a tank is sluggish or malfunctioning, not processing efficiently, the water entering the tank will begin to seek higher ground. This situation could possibly become a health hazard, not to mention the environmental stench.

Something as simple as cooking grease can clog the drainpipes of any water system but it is especially hard on septic tanks. Soaps and bleaches used in clothes washing have a tendency to destroy the bacteria that is needed inside the septic tank to break down the solid waste. Garbage disposals are not recommended for septic tanks because the waste generated by them does not easily dissolve in the tank. Some building codes specify that a larger tank must be used and extra lines added if a disposal is installed. The homebuyer who adds a disposal without additional lines may find the entire system sluggish. Any alterations to a house that affect waste water elimination could change the septic tank's ability to function properly.

If the house has both a well and a septic tank, what is the distance between them? Do the neighbors have a septic tank? What is the distance between their tank and your well? It is not advisable to have wells and septic tanks side by side.

The health department in the area has additional information on the possible effects of such a condition. Generally, a well and septic system combination is less expensive than municipal water and sewer lines, as long as they are working properly. Some periodic maintenance is required, but the well and septic tank combination can be a good, reliable system.

WATER PIPE

Houses on the market today probably have water pipes of either copper, galvanized metal, polybutalene, or a combination of these materials. Galvanized pipe probably is the oldest type, polybutalene the newest, and copper the most widely used. A house can have one kind of water pipe inside the house and another kind that brings water to the house from the outside source. This outside line is called the "service line". It can be polybutalene plastic, PVC (plastic), galvanized or copper. Pipe comes in different thicknesses. The thicker the pipe, the more pressure it can hold. Polybutalene and copper pipe will be stamped with markings that indicate the gauge and pressure capacity. You can check for these marking on a section of exposed pipe.

Galvanized pipe, usually found in older houses, has a tendency to rust. Tim Williams, a metropolitan Atlanta plumber, suggests you inspect the outside of the pipe for brown spots. These spots indicate weakness and rust. Rust can develop in galvanized pipe within a couple of weeks (while the family is on vacation, for example). Stagnation allows the pipe to rust. Continuous running water has kept the pipes "cleaned out", but when the water is off for a period of time the pipes can begin to corrode. Rust reduces the size of the opening in the pipe and in some cases closes off the pipe entirely. When the family returns from their two weeks at the shore, they might find very little water coming from some taps, perhaps no water at all from others. If you turn on the water and find that it runs slowly and is rust colored, the pipes may soon need to be replaced.

Polybutalene is a relatively new plastic. Like other plastics, it does not rust. If a polybutalene pipe is frozen, it will not split or burst. This plastic has the feature of expandability. Some reported cases of cracking probably were caused by improper installation at the joints. Other problems associated with this pipe may become evident over time, but — based on its track record to date — it appears to be a very good alternative to copper.

Copper is the most widely used water piping. Its best qualities are durability and pliability. Copper pipe comes in different thicknesses. Generally, the softer copper pipe is thicker because it has a higher copper content and less hard metal added. All solder used for the fittings for copper pipe is not the same. One type will hold more pressure than another before pulling loose at the joints or connections. Frozen copper water pipes burst, however, and this is a disadvantage. Some health authorities say that the use of copper water pipe and lead solder is dangerous to our health, because the copper and lead emit minute particles into the water and thus into our bodies. Opinions differ as to the extent of this health impact, if any. The type water in an area also has a bearing on what may happen to the water pipe (especially copper). For example, a high acid content in the water will deteriorate copper pipe. A high iron content will leave a blue stain mark in the sinks, commodes and tubs. If the house has a crawl space or basement, the pipe may be exposed. You can see what kind of pipe was used and also look for any problems or potential problems that could be costly over time.

If you are looking at a house that has been vacant during the winter, examine the pipes very carefully. If the water has been on but the heat has not, the pipes have been especially vulnerable to freezing and bursting. Any waterline that was not properly drained and/or tub, sink, and commode drain lines that were not properly winterized may have burst. And if the pipes in a vacant house are galvanized, you could find a serious rust problem.

DRAIN LINES

Drain lines are normally cast iron or plastic. They are installed with a slope, so that gravity will carry the waste from the house to the sewer or septic tank system. Too little slope and the pipe drains slowly. Too much slope and the water will not push the waste, it overruns it, leaving it behind and beginning to cause a blockage problem. In order for the drain lines to work properly, they must have vent pipes. These are the short pipes that are visible on the roof. They allow the air and gases in the drain pipes to escape so the water and waste may move freely through the pipe. Otherwise the pipes would have air blocks that would slow down the drainage. If there are not enough vents or they are not the proper size, the water also will drain slowly. These vents have flashing or rubber capping applied around them at the top of the roof so that rain water will not enter and cause a leak.

Under each fixture that drains (tubs, sinks, etc.), there is a U-shape in the pipe. This U-shape is called a "trap", and it holds water so that gases from the sewer will not come back into the house. The trap is actually a safety measure.

Stoppage in drain pipes develops for many different reasons. Usually blockage occurs at a turn or elbow in the pipe. Therefore, "cleanout" plugs are installed at various locations in the pipes in order to clean them out, if necessary, without removing all the other pipe. The main drain lines are made of cast iron, plastic, terra cotta, or some other material, depending upon the age of the house. This line should also have cleanout plugs. Buildup in the pipe can be caused by cooking grease, for example, or by flushing something like a diaper or paper towel down the commode. Sometimes blockage is caused by roots growing through the joints of a cast iron or terra cotta line that goes from the house to the main sewer or septic tank. Roots do not grow through the joints in properly installed plastic PVC or ABS pipe. If there are no trees, or signs of recently removed trees in the yard, it is not a root-related problem, and you need to investigate further.

All plastic pipe used for drain lines is not necessarily the same. A stamp on the pipe indicates the type or series, e.g., PVC or ABS. A number follows the series. The higher the number on the pipe the more pressure it can hold. For example, a number 40 pipe is thicker and stronger than a number 20. If the house was built with a crawl space or an unfinished basement, the drain pipe will be visible. You can check for any evidence of leaks. Remember, this pipe does not hold water continuously; water only runs through it periodically. You can see a leak only when the water is running through the pipe. Therefore, you need to look for signs of past leakage, not just dripping water. If the drain pipe "travels" under the driveway, you will have that repair to cope with as well if drain pipe repair or replacement becomes necessary.

The house can have a combination of pipe types. For example, a house built on a slab may have cast iron pipe under the slab, plastic above. The main point to remember in checking the appearance and function of pipes is this; if the water drains slowly and/or is discolored, there is a reason. Check all the faucets, sinks, tubs, etc. to see how well they drain. Is there a problem at one location or many? Generally, the more locations with problems the more severe the overall problem.

PLUMBING FIXTURES

Plumbing fixtures are those items which complete the plumbing work. Examples are faucets, commodes, and kitchen and bath sinks. In most houses, the most used items are the first ones to show wear and to have problems. However, unnoticed or neglected items can also cause problems or damage to the house. What are the signs to look for and what do they mean?

First, check the faucets for operation. Most people will walk all through a house and never turn on a single faucet. This is a very simple test and the results can give you vital information about the plumbing of the house. Is there sufficient water pressure at each faucet? Keep in mind that the water pressure is determined by the water pressure in the city or county main line or well pump. The size and length of the service line to the house also influences water pressure. The water pressure in the main line is not always consistent. The pressure goes up and down, depending on usage. A similar situation occurs when the pressure in one faucet goes down because more faucets are turned on. When you test the pressure at each faucet the pressure in all of them should be the same, provided no other faucet is used at the same time.

There are many reasons for low water pressure. If the pressure is less at one faucet than another, it may be because the aerator on the faucet is stopped up. The aerator is located at the head of the faucet. You can take the aerator off and check it quite easily. Another possible cause of low water pressure may be the waterlines. Waterlines leading to that particular faucet may be crimped or smaller than those going to others. The size of the pipe can be checked by looking at the line coming through the wall to serve the faucet. However, a crimped line may not be visible, just as the blockage may be hidden. If the water pressure is low and the pressure to the outside faucets is much greater, it is possible that the house has a pressure reducing valve affecting incoming water. It may need to be cleaned. The filter on the valve is probably clogged. There also is the possibility that someone has installed a water filtering system on the line. If the filters have not been changed, that could cause a slowdown in flow.

Too much pressure can be as troublesome as too little. Most newer homes have pressure reducing valves installed in the main water line. These valves keep the pressure of the water coming into the house below a certain level. The purpose of a pressure reducing valve is to protect appliances like washing machines, dishwashers, refrigerator icemakers, and other equipment not designed to handle high water pressure. High water pressure can damage these items. Outside the house it is desirable to have higher water pressure. The water pipe to outside faucets, called "seal cocks", usually branches off ahead of the pressure valve and provides maximum water pressure for such outdoor activities as washing cars and watering the lawn.

While you are testing the faucet for water pressure, you can make another quick survey. Observe the faucet to see if it drips after it has been turned off? If so, then the washers and/or valves need replacing. Even single lever faucets, which are advertised as not needing washers, etc., have a tension spring that hot water seems to loosen, causing them to leak. When this happens the spring needs to be replaced. Faucets are made of many different materials, with many different finishes, and come with a variety of design functions. Some examples are: single lever, double hand or knob, chrome, brass, and brushed brass finishes. When you are comparing houses, you should compare such amenities as these. Their costs can differ considerably.

Sinks are constructed of such materials as acrylic, steel, china, and simulated marble. As you begin to examine the sinks, check first to see if they drain properly? If not, there probably is some blockage which will need to be corrected. Blockage can be a simple problem or an extremely complex one, depending upon the location of the blockage in relation to the entire plumbing system.

While you are inspecting the kitchen and bathroom sinks, you need to look underneath. Are there water cutoff valves under these sinks? Cutoff valves allow the water to be turned off, in the event of a problem, without having to shut the water off for the entire house. Are there any signs of leaks or water damage under the sinks?

Many chronic plumbing problems develop with the drain lines and/or connections or pipe fittings. Galvanized pipes may have brown spots, indicating rust which will only continue to worsen. Any rusted pipe needs replacement. Copper pipes with obvious problems at the joints may have been soldered improperly. Problems with polybutalene pipe usually are caused by improper fittings. Are the faucets and connections on the pipe the same from bath to bath? A change may indicate a previous problem but it also may mean a quality upgrade. It may also show proper maintenance in response to normal wear.

However, ask the owner about previous leaks, faucet replacements, and any other similar problems.

Sink countertops take a lot of use and suffer a lot of abuse. Is there any swelling in the counter top around the sink? If so, water has gotten under the lip of the sink and is causing damage. It may need to be replaced because this seepage will continue to swell the countertop. At the very least, it will need to be recaulked. Sinks that fit into an opening in the countertops have a "lip". The area under and around this lip is puttied or caulked when the sink is installed. This is done to prevent water seepage. The putty may be old and the seal loose, allowing the seepage. This is a common problem in an older house, and not a serious one. The old caulk can be replaced.

Flush each commode. Does it operate properly? If it drains slowly, there may be blockage in the line. Does the water cut off completely to the commode after it has been flushed, or do you still see and hear water trickling in? If so, it may need adjusting or a new toilet tank ball. Does it have a separate water cutoff valve? If need arises the water coming to the commode can be cut off without turning the water off to the entire house. Look at the floor around the commode. Is there any water damage? If so, it probably was caused by a commode leak. Newer homes probably will have "water saver" commodes, which are commodes with smaller tanks that use less water to flush than older, standard commodes. However, don't look at this as an important water saving. There may be some saving, but many times one flush is not enough to cleanse the bowl (which is the same size as other models). The need for double flushing nearly balances the water use score card.

Tubs come in many designs, sizes, and colors.

They are made out of different materials, like fiberglass, acrylic, cast iron, steel, and simulated marble. When you look at the tub and/or shower, consider the walls around them. Do you see any water damage? If the wall is swollen at its junction with the tub, water damage is indicated. Recaulking may correct the problem, but if the swelling is very noticeable correction may require replacement of the wallboard or tile. Next, fill the tub with about six inches of water. Does the tub hold the water without any seepage? If not, the stopper system is not working and all or part of it needs to be replaced. Do the tubs and showers drain properly? There could be blockage at the stopper (hair, for example), or the cause could be a more serious problem associated with slow draining water.

You will want to check the capacity of the hot water tank to determine whether it can meet your family's needs. The condition (any previous problems with leaks?) also is important information. Does the heater look as though it might have to be replaced soon? Check around the heater for any water damaged floor that would need to be repaired or replaced. What fuels the water heater, gas or electricity? Which is the less expensive fuel in your area? You might consider the feasibility of converting to the cheaper fuel when replacement becomes necessary. Where is the hot water heater located? The best placement of a water heater is that closest to the center of the area serviced. It is more energy efficient, because less heat is lost in transit. If a gas water heater is located in the garage then no flammable materials (gasoline, paint thinner, etc.) should be stored or used in that area. The pilot light and/or burner could ignite any fumes that were present and a fire or explosion could occur. A gas water heater located in an enclosed area may need a vent of some type to obtain outside air for combustion.

Gas and electric hot water heaters have a pop-off valve on the top of the unit. This valve should be connected to a pipe which runs to the outside of the house and points downward to the ground. This pipe is a safety precaution, in case the hot water heater malfunctions and overheats the water. In the event of a malfunction the pop-off valve releases the pent up scalding water in a sudden blast, outside of the house onto the ground. The pop off valve prevents any water damage to the house. The valve also prevents the buildup of pressure from damaging the water pipes and/or fixtures. But its most important function is preventing a blow up of the heater.

Finally, taste the water. If you are making a major move — from another part of the country or from well to city water — it could taste significantly different. There might be the need for an adjustment that you had not considered. If you have an aversion to the taste you might consider a reliable filtering system. If the aversion is strong, and the taste not really correctable, you probably will want to look for another house... perhaps in a different area.

HEATING AND AIR CONDITIONING

The heating of a house can be accomplished in several ways; with a central heating system, a floor furnace, or individual room heaters which can be fueled by electricity, natural or LP gas. Steam heat is an alternative used frequently in community and multiple-dwelling buildings (e.g., apartment houses), especially in the northern United States. This type system is normally fueled by natural gas and uses a boiler with radiators in each room. Air conditioning, however, is accomplished in only two ways; with a window unit air conditioners or with a central air conditioning system. The window unit is designed to cool a specific amount of square footage. The central air conditioning system distributes cooled air through an arrangement of intake (return) and output (supply) ducts and intake (return) ducts. This same ductwork also distributes the heated air.

A house may have a solar heating (and sometimes cooling) system which is used with the other heating/ventilating/air conditioning equipment (HVAC), or possibly one that operates independently to heat and/or cool the house. Today, a totally independent solar system is still quite rare. A passive system (no motorized parts) incorporates the use of the environment to "aid " in heating or cooling. One example of passive solar is the placement of the house in a certain direction in relationship to the sun. This placement helps the sun to partially heat and light the house during the winter and to keep it cooler in the summer.

An active solar system incorporates the use of motorized equipment to aid in the heating or cooling of a house. For example, a pump which cuts on at a certain temperature and pumps a non-freezable liquid to a solar panel on the roof of a house The liquid circulates through a radiator inside the furnace which heats the air that is pushed around it by the blower on the furnace. Most solar systems use a combination of passive and active with and without the use of a storage system. An example of solar storage is hot air from a solar collector in the day time that is blown into an underground storage area filled with rocks. The air heats the rocks. At night, air from the house is circulated through the underground storage area and the rocks release the heat into the cooler air, heating the house.

DUCTWORK

When the house has central heat and/or air, the air is delivered via duct pipe. There are three types of duct pipe used in central systems: metal, flexible, and fiberglass duct board. Newer homes may have a combination of all three. Some ducts supply air to each room and others return air back to the unit. These ducts can be in the floor or ceiling. The supply ducts (output) should be wrapped with insulation and the joints tightly sealed with duct tape so that no air (heated or cooled) is lost through the ductwork. All this taping and insulation make for a much more energy efficient system. In order for the central air system to work properly there should be at least one high return for hot air intake which can then be cooled, and one low return for cool air which can then be heated.

The size of the ducts is important because it determines the amount of air to each room. Air can be restricted by elbows or turns in the duct work. Vents are placed in each room where the duct pipe enters. Vent openings should be adjustable, so the system can be balanced from season to season. Adjustable vents allow you to control the volume of air that enters each room. This feature enables you to keep one room — or one story — warmer or cooler than the rest of the house. In a two-story house, the vent(s) in the second story could be adjusted in the winter (because hot air rises). In the summer, the first story vents could be adjusted — because cold air settles. This is called "balancing the system" and it is done to maintain a more even temperature throughout the whole house.

Ratings: Gas and Electric Equipment

Over the past several years the term "energy efficient" has enjoyed wide and popular usage. The efficiency rating of equipment is important; the more efficient, the lower its operating cost. Today's electrical equipment has the SEER (Seasonal Energy Efficient Rate) ratings. The higher the SEER number, the more efficiently the equipment will operate. For example, a unit with a rating of 8 will cost more to operate than one with a rating of 12. With gas equipment, the efficiency rating is stated as a percentage. A gas furnace with a 65% rating, for example, will cost more to operate than one rated at 90%; 35% of the heat gained from burning the gas is lost with a 65% furnace, but only 10% is lost with a 90% unit.

Almost as important as the efficiency of the equipment is the type fuel that is being used. What fuels the fire? About fifteen years ago the term "Total Electric" was aggressively promoted in the south. Today, the owners of those same houses are paying a penalty for the amount of electricity consumed. You could have a high efficiency electric furnace that would cost more to operate than a lower efficiency gas furnace if the cost for electricity is higher than gas in that area. The local Public Service Commission should be able to provide you with five to ten year projections on fuel costs so you can consider what is best for you, now and in the future.

When you are trying to evaluate fuel costs you will need to convert the information you receive into usable information. LP and natural gas furnaces are sized in BTU's (British Thermal Units); electrical furnaces by KWs (kilowatts).

To find the BTU equivalents you multiply 3.414 X the KW's. Then take this figure and multiply it times your cost per fuel unit. If the answer confuses more than it enlightens, you can call the utility company, or — the most direct approach — ask the owner to show you the last year's month-by-month bills.

EQUIPMENT

When you inspect the equipment itself, check it first for age and placement within the house. The age of the equipment is an important factor. Not only will older equipment require replacement sooner, newer equipment probably is more efficient. The location of the heating and cooling equipment is equally important. If the furnace is located at the center of the house, rather than to one side or the other, the air will flow more easily through the ducts with less temperature gain or loss.

A vertical furnace is normally more efficient than the same type furnace in a horizontal configuration and it usually carries a longer warranty on the heat exchanger. The heat exchanger is that part of a gas furnace that separates the gas that is being burned from the air that is being heated. A furnace located within the house is more efficient than one in a crawl space. And a furnace located within a house is safer if it has an outside air vent for combustion. This is a vent that uses air from the outside rather than burning the oxygen in the air inside the house. All gas equipment should have a cutoff valve located close to the equipment so the gas can be cut off, if necessary.

The life span of a furnace for central heating depends on the environment in which it is located and the maintenance that is performed. The average life span of a central unit is approximately 15 to 20 years. However, floor furnaces, with proper maintenance, can last between 35 and 40 years. Every gas furnace has a vent that goes to the outside of the house, normally through the roof, which vents the poisonous gases emitted by the burning of the gas. This vent should be checked by a professional whenever the equipment is serviced (at least annually) to be sure that these vapors are discharging completely.

All gas furnaces have some type of pilot light or ignition system. Some have electronic ignition, which means that an electric spark ignites the gas. Gas and electric central furnaces and/or air conditioners have air filters which should be cleaned or exchanged several times during the heating and cooling seasons. A dirty air filter restricts air movement; as a result, the furnace or air conditioning unit will not heat or cool as it should. A dirty filter on an electrical furnace can cause the heating elements to overheat and cease to function because of the restricted air flow.

Gas and electric central furnaces with air conditioning have a condensation line. This line allows the water that is taken from the house air, during the cooling process, to drain outside or into a plumbing drain line. This line should be inspected to ensure it is not stopped up. Such stoppage would cause the water to drain back into the unit, eventually rusting it.

Both the gas and electric central air systems use freon. There is a freon line that runs from the furnace coil inside the furnace to the air condenser outside. The freon gas in the system cools the air. Too little freon and the unit does not cool properly. Too much will cause the compressor to blow. Freon must remain "in balance." If the homeowner has been adding freon to the unit every year, there is a leak. Freon leaks can be expensive to repair. Ask the owner about any problems with the freon. The air conditioning system will work best with the shortest possible distance of the freon line from the furnace to the air condenser outside the house. Gas floor furnaces and electric baseboard heat are not connected to a duct system. With this kind of heating system in place, air conditioning must be accomplished with window units.

The thermostat should be centrally located and not close to any supply or return vents. Air currents from adjacent or nearby vents and ducts will influence the temperature reading of the thermostat and will cause the system to cycle on and off more than normal. Contrary to popular belief, sharply lowering the thermostat to cool the house more quickly does not work. An air conditioning system will cool the air inside the house by only a few degrees at a time and then return it. For example, if the temperature inside the house is 80 degrees, and the thermostat is set at 70 degrees, the unit will cool the 80 degrees air between 14 and 18 degrees and return it. This cooled air then mixes with the remaining air. The process is repeated until the thermostat registers that all the air in the house has been cooled to 70 degrees. If the temperature setting was moved to 50 degrees, the unit would still only cool the 80 degree air 14 to 18 degrees and return it. This cycle would repeat until the desired temperature was achieved but setting the thermostat at 50 degrees does not immediately deliver 50 degree cooled air. Cooling air is done in "degrees", a step-by-step process that significantly lower thermostat settings will not accelerate.

The size of the heating and cooling unit is determined by the square footage of the house and the heat gain and loss factor. Heat gain does not refer to heat that is artificially made but to the actual amount of heat that the house absorbs from the outside, through the windows, walls, ceiling, etc. This effects the cooling of the house. Heat loss is just the reverse; simply put, it is the amount of heat that the house loses by the same means. Heat loss and gain are influenced by such things as insulation, windows, doors and drapes. These factors, along with the cost of fuel for the unit, (and the degree to which you and your family like the house heated or cooled) will determine the overall cost for utilities.

Most professionals agree that it is cheaper to size the equipment to run longer than to have a larger unit cycling on and off. If you know the size of the unit(s) and the square footage of the house a professional can advise you of the most efficient equipment size. If you are anticipating a room addition, then the size and age of the equipment is even more important. The existing equipment may not be able to heat or cool the additional space. Sometimes, the house can be insulated better and the existing equipment is able to accommodate the extra space. If not, there may be only two choices: to buy a larger piece of equipment that can handle the new load or to add a separate system that heats and/or cools the addition independently.

Gas furnaces should have a safety check every year, before start-up for the new heating season. This checkup should be done by a professional. The heat exchanger is a metal casing that separates burning gas from the inside air it is heating. If the heat exchanger is cracked, it will allow poisonous gases to enter the house. The burner should be cleaned by a professional for an equally compelling reason; if it stops up, it could cause a delay in ignition which could cause an explosion. The safety controls should be checked for proper operation and the motor oiled for longer life.

Nevertheless, most furnaces are not checked each year, only when there is an apparent problem. Ask the owner when the furnace was last checked and by whom. A professional inspection is the only safe, acceptable checkup. If you are in doubt about any aspect of the gas or electrical equipment you should contact a professional. This is not an area in which unqualified opinions should be accepted.

ELECTRICAL

The electrical inspection of an older house is one of the most important items on the entire house checklist. New, never occupied, homes are insured to a degree by the building codes. These codes require that certain quality standards be met or the house will not be cleared for occupancy.

Houses use alternating current (AC). Lights and motors for equipment are designed to operate on this current. Electricity enters the house at the meter, which measures the amount of electricity used. Then it travels through the main service line to the panel box, which has either fuses or circuit breakers. From this box electricity is distributed through the house by electrical wires to: electrical equipment, like a dishwasher; light switches; lights and receptacles (which are wall plugs TV sets, radios, and small appliances), etc.

WIRING

It is not unusual for a municipality's electrical inspector to require the entire rewiring of an older house before it can be occupied by the new owner. Generally speaking, older homes were not designed to accommodate the needs of today's lifestyle (multiple TV sets, VCRs, stereo systems, electric guitars and amplifiers, hair dryers, microwaves, etc.). The new demand on the old wiring and fuse box system can place the entire wiring of the house, and implicitly the house itself, in jeopardy.

Wiring for a house is grounded, to either the copper cold water piping or to a ground rod, for the purpose of discharging any fault current (lightning, for example). A ground rod should be located outside of the house near the panel box. You should check the ground rod to be sure that it is not corroding. A corroded ground rod can not divert the fault current, so it goes back into the wiring of the house. An important safety precaution: do not attempt to disconnect the ground rod for the purpose of cleaning unless the main fuse or breaker is off.

There are three types of wire that have been and

are being used in house electrical wiring today. They are copper, copper clad, and aluminum. Normally, the main service line is aluminum and the rest of the wiring copper. The size of the wire determines the amount of electricity that can travel through it. Different sizes of wires are used for different applications in a house. For example, a number 12 wire is used for lighting, a number 10 wire for the clothes dryer.

According to Hoyt Swaney, the Director of Permits and Licensing in Clayton County, Georgia, aluminum wire has been banned from use as the wire for wall plugs and lights because of problems concerning its lack of pliability and durability. The aluminum wiring has had conductive problems. These have lead to dangerous arcing, and that has precipitated a number of house fires. Aluminum wire was popularly used because it was cheaper. It has now been proven to be unsafe. We suggest you walk away from a house that has total aluminum wiring. Its poor safety record underscores that suggestion.

Copper clad wire is aluminum wire with a copper coating. If you look at it from the outside, it appears to be copper but when you look at the tip you can see the aluminum in the center. Copper clad wire does not seem to suffer from any problems associated with the 100% aluminum wire.

Electricians and builders use copper clad wire because it is cost effective; i.e., cheaper than 100% copper wire. However, the more expensive 100% copper wire is the most dependable. Copper wire is pliable, durable and therefore very reliable. A house that has all copper wiring is your best choice.

You can see the wiring of the house in most attics, unfinished basements, or crawl spaces. You will want to check the covering for shredding or peeling. Any wire that exhibits such problems will require replacement. If any wire is loose or hanging, it should be secured. In the areas where the wiring is exposed, you may be able to feel the outside casing of the wires that supply equipment like clothes dryers or air conditioners. You want to feel for any warmth after the equipment has been running for a while. If the wire is warm, you have a problem; it could be that the wire is not sized correctly or that the equipment is going to break down. Whatever the cause, the wire should not feel warm. The wiring of the entire house needs further investigation.

If there is one area of a house that suggests you solicit professional advice, it is the electrical wiring. If you are in doubt about any aspect of the house's electrical service, call a professional for consultation before giving the house further consideration.

PANEL BOX

All the wiring for the entire house comes together at the panel box. Panel boxes either have fuses or circuit breakers, with fuses typically found in older homes. Most new homes have a circuit breaker panel box. The principal is the same for either box. When the demand for electrical power is too great for the wiring connected to a specific fuse or circuit breaker, the fuse will blow or the breaker will "kick off".

The fuse box has a series of fuses which act as safety insurance against electrical overloads. Fuses are numbered according to the amount of electricity (amps) the fuse allows to pass. For example, the lighting fuses are a lower number than the fuse that controls the kitchen appliances. When a fuse "blows" it should be replaced with the exact same size. A problem can arise when the homeowner replaces a smaller size fuse with a larger fuse than the wire at that fuse socket can handle. In the "old days" (some still do it), people put a copper penny behind the fuse to reconnect the blown fuse. This is a very dangerous practice because it frustrates the safety purpose of the fuse. A fuse blows in an effort to prevent too much electricity from being drawn through the wire. Any wire carrying more current than it was designed to handle can burn and possibly start a fire, rather than blowing a fuse — as it is supposed to do.

When used properly, fuse boxes are safe. Ask the owner if he has had continuing problems with any fuses blowing. Since this type panel box is in use primarily in older homes, chronic problems may be an indication that the wiring and/or panel box needs replacing. Rewiring an older home is a major, additional investment to consider.

The circuit breaker panel box has switches that are similar to light switches in design, but much sturdier. Circuit breakers come in different amp sizes, just like fuses. When the demand for electricity exceeds the supply, the circuit breaker "kicks off". Actually, the switch flips off and no electricity is delivered through that particular breaker. The most common cause for circuit breakers kicking off is the simultaneous use of too many kitchen appliances (particularly those of the heat-generating variety), which places too great a demand on the breaker; so it kicks, as it is designed to do.

To remedy the situation the occupant must first reduce the demand, then flip the circuit breaker switch back to the "On" position. When you open and look at the panel box, it is easy to see which circuit has kicked off. All the breakers that are working are in one position. The breaker that has kicked off is in the opposite position.

When you inspect either type of panel box, feel the fuses or breakers for warmth. They should not be warm. A warm fuse or breaker is a warning that the electrical system is not functioning as it should. Ask the owner if any additional lines have been brought into the panel box. All electrical work at the panel box — or anywhere else in the house — should be done by a professional.

Consider the electrical appliances that the present family uses. Will your family use more? If you plan a room addition, the size of the panel box may need to be increased to accommodate the new demand. Such a change could be expensive. Any problem, or impending change of any type, is a signal for you to consult a professional before considering the house any further.

SWITCHES & RECEPTACLES

Switches are designed to make and break connections in the electrical circuit. There are standard on/off switches and there are button switches. A popular variation of the button switch is the dimmer switch. Button switches function by making or breaking the electrical connection. A dimmer switch provides infinitely variable degrees of lighting by allowing varying amounts of electrical current through the circuit. You should turn the switches on and off to see that they operate properly. Do you see any sparks from the switch when it is turned on? That indicates either that the switch is beginning to fail and/or that the wiring is not making a good connection. This particular switch may need to be replaced.

Receptacles always "ON" — in other words, ready to deliver electricity — unlike the switch, which can be "ON" or "OFF". A wall receptacle will pass electricity through whatever conductive material is placed into its socket, whether it is an appropriate conductor (like a hair dryer), or an inappropriate conductor (like a hair pin). You can use an inexpensive nightlight to test the receptacles. Any wall receptacle that appears damaged (burned or smoke stained) will need to be replaced. Either something has caused the damage, or the receptacle or wiring is going bad.

Plugging in an appliance that has already been turned "On" is another reason for damaged receptacles. Anytime this is done, the receptacle and/or appliance will arc in an effort to make connection. All appliances or items that require electricity should be in the "Off" position when plugged into the socket. When you check out the receptacles you also want to look for changes and additions. Ask the owner about alterations in the electrical system. Will it be necessary for you to add any receptacles? Older houses have a limited number, and it is very dangerous to overload them. Any outside receptacles, as well as outside lights, should be waterproof and weather tight.

In older homes there may be a problem when an old receptacle has been replaced with a newer one. The older receptacle probably had only two holes to deliver electricity to an appliance, but the replacement has three holes — with the third being a grounding wire. Simply replacing the receptacle does not provide any grounding. Neither does a "pigtail" adapter. The pigtail only enables the two hole receptacle to accept a three-pronged plug. Here again, no grounding is provided.

You will need to look at each receptacle in an older house. If all the receptacles are three-holed, it's likely all the receptacles are grounded. If only some are, you may want to have an electrician undo each three-hole receptacle to be sure each has three wires.

ELECTRICAL FIXTURES

Fixtures include items like: door bells and chimes; all fans, including bath, exhaust, attic, and ceiling fans, with or without lights; smoke and heat detectors; and of course all lighting fixtures. When you inspect the house, you should check all the lighting fixtures to make sure they are working and that they are safely secured to the ceiling or wall. Replacement lighting fixtures should have a ground wire to discharge any build up in current (fault current). Closet lights should be at least eighteen inches from the walls or shelves.

When you check the lighting fixtures you need to see what size bulbs are being used. The bulb size should not exceed the manufacturer's recommendation, because the wire in the fixture is designed to carry only a specific amount of electricity. A very common problem with older homes is overloading of light fixtures with higher wattage bulbs. This practice can damage the wiring because of the excessive heat buildup over time. If the present owner has been oversizing the lighting fixtures they may soon need replacing. You can find out the correct wattage to be used by looking for the manufacturer's recommendation on the fixture. Another problem with light bulbs is premature burning out. Light bulbs should burn for a specified number of hours. When they repeatedly burn out well before that time, there is a problem with the electrical system. The problem could even be a surge of electricity caused by a bad transformer at the street or the location of the house at the end of the powerline (e.g., a dead end street). Problems of this type are the responsibility of the power company and they should be brought to the utility's attention. Don't hesitate to ask the owner about any such problems.

Usually there are no problems with the door bell or chimes. They should work properly; if not, they should be replaced. If there is a problem, it usually is the button or the transformer that needs replacing. This is a simple task, one with which many laymen can cope.

All fans in the house should be inspected, including bath fans. Attic exhaust fans should work efficiently (and relatively quietly) and have a shutter that closes when the fan is not being used. Ceiling fans and any combined fan/lighting fixtures also should be checked. A light on a ceiling fan needs to have a separate switch (often a pull chain).

Smoke detectors can either be battery-operated or connected to the house wiring. A smoke detector should be set off by any small amount of smoke. A smoke detector has a filter that requires periodic cleaning. If it is battery operated, the battery must be replaced regularly. Heat detectors or sensors react to heat rather than smoke. Very few houses have these detectors but if they do, they should be located near major appliances or equipment; i.e., stoves, furnaces, and hot water heaters. You can check the sensitivity of heat detectors with a lit match.

Checklist #4: Plumbing, Electrical, Heating, and Air Conditioning

	House #1 Location:_____	NO PROBLEM	MINIMUM	MINOR	MAJOR	HOLD
		0	1	2	3	?
1	Are you satisfied with the water system?					
2	If there is a well, will it supply your needs?					
3	Has the owner had any trouble with the well?					
4	Does the house have a septic tank? Have there been problems?					
5	Will you need to tap into sewer? Is a sewer line available?					
6	Did you see rust colored water coming from any faucets?					
7	Are all water pipes in satisfactory condition?					
8	Have there been any problems with the drain lines and/or drainage?					
9	Do all the water faucets work properly?					
10	Are the sinks and tubs draining without any problems?					
11	Will any countertops need repair or replacement?					
12	Has there been any trouble with the toilets?					
13	Do all the tubs and showers work properly?					
14	Have there been any problems with the hot water heater?					
15	Will the hot water heater need repair or replacement?					
16	Are there sufficient air vents for the central air system? Adjustable?					
17	Does the house have energy efficient equipment?					
18	Does the equipment use the least expensive fuel for your area?					
19	Are the present utility bills acceptable for your budget?					
20	Has the gas furnace had an annual professional checkup?					
21	Have the filters and drain lines for the furnace been maintained?					
22	Have there been persistent problems with the freon in the central air unit?					
23	When was the gas furnace last cleaned?					
24	Are there any indications that the house may need rewiring?					
25	Are any fuses or circuit breakers warm to the touch? DANGER					
26	Will any switches or receptacles need replacing?					
27	Do all lighting fixtures operate properly?					
28	Is there any evidence of past overloading of lighting fixtures?					
29	REMARKS OR OTHER:					
30						

TRANSFER SUB-TOTALS TO
MASTER CHECKLIST FORM

SUB-TOTAL

ADDITIONAL REMARKS OR OTHERS:

_____

_____

_____

_____

_____

_____

_____

_____

_____

_____

_____

_____

_____

_____

Checklist #4: Plumbing, Electrical, Heating, and Air Conditioning

House #2

Location:_____

		NO PROBLEM	MINIMUM	MINOR	MAJOR	HOLD
		0	1	2	3	?
1	Are you satisfied with the water system?					
2	If there is a well, will it supply your needs?					
3	Has the owner had any trouble with the well?					
4	Does the house have a septic tank? Have there been problems?					
5	Will you need to tap into sewer? Is a sewer line available?					
6	Did you see rust colored water coming from any faucets?					
7	Are all water pipes in satisfactory condition?					
8	Have there been any problems with the drain lines and/or drainage?					
9	Do all the water faucets work properly?					
10	Are the sinks and tubs draining without any problems?					
11	Will any countertops need repair or replacement?					
12	Has there been any trouble with the toilets?					
13	Do all the tubs and showers work properly?					
14	Have there been any problems with the hot water heater?					
15	Will the hot water heater need repair or replacement?					
16	Are there sufficient air vents for the central air system? Adjustable?					
17	Does the house have energy efficient equipment?					
18	Does the equipment use the least expensive fuel for your area?					
19	Are the present utility bills acceptable for your budget?					
20	Has the gas furnace had an annual professional checkup?					
21	Have the filters and drain lines for the furnace been maintained?					
22	Have there been persistent problems with the freon in the central air unit?					
23	When was the gas furnace last cleaned?					
24	Are there any indications that the house may need rewiring?					
25	Are any fuses or circuit breakers warm to the touch? DANGER					
26	Will any switches or receptacles need replacing?					
27	Do all lighting fixtures operate properly?					
28	Is there any evidence of past overloading of lighting fixtures?					
29	REMARKS OR OTHER:					
30						
	SUB-TOTAL					

TRANSFER SUB-TOTALS TO
MASTER CHECKLIST FORM

ADDITIONAL REMARKS OR OTHERS:

_____

_____

_____

_____

_____

_____

_____

_____

_____

_____

_____

_____

_____

_____

_____

_____

_____

Checklist #4: Plumbing, Electrical, Heating, and Air Conditioning

	House #3 Location:_____	NO PROBLEM	MINIMUM	MINOR	MAJOR	HOLD
		0	1	2	3	?
1	Are you satisfied with the water system?					
2	If there is a well, will it supply your needs?					
3	Has the owner had any trouble with the well?					
4	Does the house have a septic tank? Have there been problems?					
5	Will you need to tap into sewer? Is a sewer line available?					
6	Did you see rust colored water coming from any faucets?					
7	Are all water pipes in satisfactory condition?					
8	Have there been any problems with the drain lines and/or drainage?					
9	Do all the water faucets work properly?					
10	Are the sinks and tubs draining without any problems?					
11	Will any countertops need repair or replacement?					
12	Has there been any trouble with the toilets?					
13	Do all the tubs and showers work properly?					
14	Have there been any problems with the hot water heater?					
15	Will the hot water heater need repair or replacement?					
16	Are there sufficient air vents for the central air system? Adjustable?					
17	Does the house have energy efficient equipment?					
18	Does the equipment use the least expensive fuel for your area?					
19	Are the present utility bills acceptable for your budget?					
20	Has the gas furnace had an annual professional checkup?					
21	Have the filters and drain lines for the furnace been maintained?					
22	Have there been persistent problems with the freon in the central air unit?					
23	When was the gas furnace last cleaned?					
24	Are there any indications that the house may need rewiring?					
25	Are any fuses or circuit breakers warm to the touch? DANGER					
26	Will any switches or receptacles need replacing?					
27	Do all lighting fixtures operate properly?					
28	Is there any evidence of past overloading of lighting fixtures?					
29	REMARKS OR OTHER:					
30						

TRANSFER SUB-TOTALS TO
MASTER CHECKLIST FORM

SUB-TOTAL

ADDITIONAL REMARKS OR OTHERS:

_____

_____

_____

_____

_____

_____

_____

_____

_____

_____

_____

_____

5: Roofing, Insulation, and Interior Walls

Chapter five will help you examine some of the basic structural elements of the house; the roof, the walls, and the ceilings. Descriptions of insulation and of energy efficiency also are included.

ROOFING

The style of the roof and the composition of the roofing material are important elements in the overall design of the house. There are many roof styles and a great variety of roofing materials. Often the name given to a roof style is the name associated with that style house. You can probably see in your mind's eye a picture of the roof when you hear English Tudor or A-Frame.

However, you will be more concerned with the condition of the roof than you will with its style. You will want to know how old it is? Has the roof been patched? The house reroofed? When? Will you have to face the cost of a new roof soon after you take occupancy? If so, how much would that cost?

ROOF DESIGN

The style of the roof completes the design of a house. Many houses, like an English Tudor or French Provincial, are distinguished by their roof lines. Often it is the pitch (height) of the roof that determines a specific roof style. A authentic

Spanish style house will have terra cotta roofing (clay shingles) with a pitch that is rather flat while. A Contemporary may have a cedar shake roof with sharp roof line angles. Many houses of the late fifties and early sixties are distinguished by the (then) "Modern" look of a flat roof.

TYPES OF ROOFING MATERIALS

The fiberglass shingle is the most common roofing material being used on new homes. It is available in many different colors and with a number of designs. Some designs are cut and colored to simulate the look of slate or cedar shake roofing (much more expensive roofing materials). Fiberglass shingles have a center of fiberglass mesh that is topped with a colored aggregate and based with a tar mixture. The fiberglass center binds the shingle together. Asphalt shingles are similar, but the binding center is paper. Roll roofing is the same composition of either fiberglass or asphalt, but it is formed in a roll. The roll is applied like felt, with tar at the edges. Roll roofing is used for very low sloped roofs.

Slate, clay tile, and terra cotta are heavier materials. They require a sturdy, very strong roof system to support the additional weight. A "Flat" roof also will require a strong roof system, as will a "Built-Up" roof. A built-up roof is another name for a flat roof; the tar and felt are layered together several times, before the gravel is added to finish the roof. The flat roof usually has a metal edge around the perimeter to keep any loose gravel from washing off during a heavy rain.

Cedar shakes are made from pieces of wood that have been machine or hand split. These shakes are lapped when they are put in place on the roof. Usually a layer of felt is placed on the back portion of the shake before the next row of shakes is applied.

APPLICATION

Roofing material is counted in squares, with one square designed to cover one hundred square feet. A shingle is one piece of roofing, whether it is fiberglass, asphalt, wood shake, or slate.

Regardless of the roofing material used, most roofs are built in the same way, following the same steps. First, the wood underpart of the roof, called decking, is covered with felt. This step is called "drying in", because the felt will keep out the rain for at least a limited time. Then a starter run is put in place. This starter run covers the felt at the roof line and helps keep rain out permanently. When the roofing is applied properly you can see uniformity throughout the entire roof. Whether you look at the top (ridge), the sides, or the bottom, the distances between the shingles are equal.

COLOR

After you inspect the roof for uniformity in application, look for continuity in color. Roofing is produced in batches, with each batch assigned a number. They may only be slight (perhaps a subtle change in the shade of grey), but there are differences in color from one batch of the same brand/color/design roofing to the next. If the roof

has been patched rather than completely reroofed you will probably see the difference because a color change usually means some patching was done after the roof was originally installed. Ask the owner what caused the need for the repair. Many times a problem that required patching resurfaces somewhere else at a later date. Unless you are wealthy beyond description and are evaluating a number of residential properties just to keep your eyes sharp and your brain alert, ask for the reasons behind every significant repair. Otherwise your "closing costs" might continue long after you move in.

COLOR

Color also is important as an energy factor. A black roof absorbs much more heat than a white roof. To achieve maximum energy efficiency benefit, the color should be matched to the climate. For example, white roofs in Florida are very efficient because they reflect the sun's rays and assist, in a passive solar way, in keeping the temperature down inside the house. Similarly, a black roof in Minnesota will help to retain heat gain.

GUARANTEES

Even though there may not have been any obvious repairs to the roof, you will want to know the specifics of any warranty that may still be in effect. How many years are left on the warranty? Is the prorated replacement clause based on the present cost of labor and materials or the cost at the time of original purchase? The roofing shingles must have been installed according to the manufacturer's recommendations, or the warranty will have been violated.

REROOFING

There are certain signs that will alert you to the need for a new roof. If the roofing is turning up at the edges, cracking, or blistering, a new roof in the near future is probable. If the roofing material is cedar shakes, you may have to replace the cracked shakes only. If there is more general deterioration of the shakes, however, the entire roof may have to be replaced. In a clay tile roof, the tiles that are cracked will have to be replaced. Anytime any exposed felt is visible, the roof has a problem that needs attention.

In most cases of reroofing, the new roof is installed over the old roof. There is a limit, however, to the number of layers of roofing material a house structure can support. Houses are built to carry defined weight loads. Too much added weight can effect the overall support. If you are looking at an older house and wondering how many new roofs have been placed since the house was built, you can count them at the edge. The number may need to be divided by two If the number seems unreasonably high, divide it by two. For example, six layers of roofing is apt to mean that a starter run was used at the edge each time the house was reroofed. The actual number of roofs that have been applied is three. If it appears that a new roof will be required, bear in mind the cost of reroofing is influenced (upward) by the steepness of the roof and whether old roofing must be removed.

SKYLIGHTS

Skylight design has improved in recent years. Used originally for aesthetic reasons only (style, not function), skylights today are used for the light that they supply as well as the style that they add. Now an improved product in many respects, skylights are available double paned, tinted, and insulated. Many variations are offered, such as a motor to open and close the skylight. Others are hand operated.

The biggest problem with any skylight is leaks. It almost seems that some leakage is inevitable as,

over time, the caulking sealing the skylight cracks. Replacement of the caulking is not a difficult job, especially if you remove as much of the old caulking as possible before applying the new. If you see water stains around the skylight, or other evidence of leakage, ask the owner if the caulking sealing the skylight has been repaired. If not, this item should be added to your owner's "fix-it" list. Even slight leaks can cause wood to rot eventually, so all leaks should be repaired - and so should the secondary damage caused by the leaks.

INSULATION

Insulation alone does not make a house energy efficient. Proper insulation only aids in the retention of heat or cold, and is just one of the factors that determine the energy efficiency of a particular house.

Insulation must work against two opposing forces; the outside temperature trying to penetrate the house and the inside temperature trying to escape. The purpose of insulating material is to extend the time these forces normally take to affect adversely the ambient temperature inside the house, thus keeping the house cooler or warmer, as desired, for a longer period of time.

Just as an open window hinders the heating or cooling in a room, cracks and other openings in a house also allow outside air to penetrate, with the same effect. On the other hand a house can be too airtight. Houses need to have a exchange of air to allow normal vapors and fumes to be exhausted. Proper air movement also helps materials adjust to humidity and temperature changes. When this air movement is not possible, it should be created by some other means.

Many of today's insulating products were not available just a few years ago. Most older houses will not have the wall or floor insulation of newer homes because building codes then did not require them. Even today some new homes do not have floor insulation; either it is not a requirement and/or the climate does not require it. Also, fuel was relatively cheap a generation or two ago, so the need for insulating products was not as compelling. Such is not the case today. As the need for cost efficiency in home heating and cooling systems manifested itself, more and better insulating products were produced. Now a variety of insulation products and materials are available, and the "R" rating is king.

RATINGS

Insulating materials are rated with an "R" factor. This factor is expressed numerically, with a higher number indicating more insulation. R-30 insulation is better than an R-26. All areas of the house do not require the same insulation. Because more heat loss or gain is realized through the ceiling and/or roof than through the walls or floor, the ceiling needs the more effective insulation.

TYPES

You will find insulation products in many different types, qualities, and thicknesses. Four inches of one product is not necessarily equal to four inches of another. You can have two products of the same thickness, and the R value of one will be twice that of the other. A house usually is insulated with more than one type of insulating material. A typical home might have sheet insulation and batting for exterior walls, batting for floors and some ceilings, and blown insulation for attics and ceilings.

Sometimes you can tell if insulation has been added to the exterior walls of an older brick house. It may be evident on examination that bricks near the roof have been removed, and then replaced, every sixteen inches or so. They were removed so that foam insulation could be injected between the walls. Very popular in the seventies, this was done to houses that had little or no wall insulation put in place when the house was constructed.

Unfortunately, there were problems with the formaldehyde used in some of the formulas. Many people found they were allergic to it. If you suspect that foam insulation might have been injected into the older house you are looking at, you probably will want to have any such insulating material analyzed. While adding the insulation after the house had been built was not an easy task, removing it is next to impossible. If you, and/or your family, might be sensitive to formaldehyde or other chemicals, you probably would be well served by avoiding a house with this kind of insulation. Ask the owner for clear and specific answers if you suspect that the house has been so insulated.

About energy efficiency (again)...When you are looking at houses, keep in mind that whatever level of energy efficiency the house enjoys is determined by the accumulated effectiveness of all the insulating measures taken. This aggregate most accurately reflects the house's ability to use energy efficiently. For example, an ad describing a house for sale may refer to "Insulated Doors and Windows". But then, when you go to the subdivision to look, you see blackboard sheathing on the sides of the house. Blackboard sheathing is one of the cheapest insulating boards in use. Its R value is low, compared to a styrofoam sheathing of the same thickness. The insulated doors and windows are a plus, but because of the negative effect of poor wall insulation, the overall energy efficiency score may be low. If you are unable to see the type of sheathing that has been used on a house you are inspecting, try to look at the other houses being built by the same contractor. A builder normally uses the same products on each house. If you are not able to check in that way, ask the real estate agent, builder, or owner for the information you need.

AIR VENTILATION

Contrary to popular opinion, packing insulation very tightly does not improve the R factor. Tight packing actually has a negative impact on insulation effectiveness. Since air itself is an insulator, air space adds to the insulating factor. Insulated windows have an air space between the two layers of glass. To appreciate the insulating quality of air space, think about a down comforter or jacket. These products are very warm - and very light. The air space enhances the ability of the down to insulate.

Air space is especially vital to the roof and ceiling. Most of the temperature change a house suffers is gained or lost through the roof. Even vaulted ceilings need insulation and air space. Baffles, a U-shaped styrofoam product, are used above the insulation on the decking of the roof over a vaulted ceiling. They create an air space. Since the vaulted ceiling has no attic space, an air space is formed between the bottom of the roof decking and the insulating material. The air space allows for air circulation which helps remove the heat buildup, as it circulates, cools down, and gives off heat that tries to penetrate to the inside. If there were no air space the heat would build up and bleed through the insulation into the house much more quickly.

Air spaces also help composition roofing shingles, which otherwise would bake and crack from the underside and deteriorate much sooner. Houses also have power vents at the roof, gable, and cornice which provide additional air movement to help to keep the temperature down.

Check the cornice, gable(s), and roof for vents. If there are no vents, and the house is at least ten years old, the roof probably has started to deteriorate. It also costs more to heat and cool a house that has no such vents.

Air space is important under the house as well. If a house is built on a crawl space, it should have foundation vents with shutters. The vent can be opened in the summer to provide additional circulating, cooling air and closed in the winter to cut down on cooling drafts and help prevent frozen pipes. Foundation vents help to prevent normal sweating because they allow air to keep circulating. The ground is constantly giving off moisture and this circulating air speeds evaporation.

A few words about Radon would be appropriate here. A new study released in January, 1988 by the National Academy of Sciences (NAS), confirms the significance of Radon as a cause of lung cancer. If you suspect Radon (a colorless, odorless gas) may be a problem in your area, check with the county extension agent or any other appropriate government office. The NAS estimates that 13,000 cases of lung cancer per year are attributable to Radon in homes.

If you walk into a vacant house that has not had any heating or cooling equipment operating for an extended period, you can estimate the efficiency of the house's insulation by noting the difference between the outside and inside temperatures. If the difference is distinct, (e.g., the house is relatively cool on a hot summer day), the house's insulation is working effectively. If the difference is minimal, the house's insulation probably is poor. It is no secret that energy efficiency is directly reflected in power company and/or fuel delivery bills. It is always a good idea to ask the owner what his month-by-month energy costs have been over the past year.

WALLS

Chances are the walls of the house are in acceptable condition. When the walls have such obvious defects that you are concerned about the rest of the house, your thoughts probably are well-founded. Walls with severe problems - like cracks in the sheetrock - point to some structural deficiency; deficiencies like cracked foundations and sagging roofs. Your main concern then is to determine whether the wall problem that disturbs you actually is structural.

Wall bows are a relatively minor problems. Bows develop when a piece of wood (wood that probably should not have been used by the builder) used to make the wall has a crown or high point. Most of the time problems with the walls are aesthetical rather than structural. You are entitled to expect walls to be plumb (vertically level). If an item as simple as a wall has not been done correctly, you are likely to find more severe problems elsewhere. Since walls are composites of other materials you will find further discussion of each part (and problems pertinent to those parts) in the following paragraphs. You may also want to refer again to the material on framing in chapter two.

SHEETROCK

Most interior walls and ceilings are constructed of sheetrock, also referred to as drywall. Sheetrock is gypsum, sold in 4' by 8' and 4' by 12' sheets, and used exclusively in the construction of walls and ceilings. There are different thicknesses of sheetrock, but most walls are built with one-half inch thick material. Some sheetrock is rated for its fire resistance qualities.

When sheetrock is installed, the sheetrock boards are nailed and/or glued to the wooden studs of the wall. Then all the joints are taped with a special paper tape. The tape and nails are covered with a joint compound (also called sheetrock "mud"). Several coats, usually three, are applied, dried individually, and then sanded smooth. This sanding prepares the wall for paint or wallpaper.

Sometimes a board of sheetrock is not nailed properly. You can check for this problem by slightly bumping the sheetrock with the palm of your hand. If the sheetrock rattles, it is loose; the rattling noise the sheetrock vibrating against the wall studs. You may want to check for loose sheetrock randomly throughout the house. This is a particularly valid check in a new home, where you should expect all the sheetrock to be properly secured. The correction is to nail, re-apply joint compound, and repaint. Although loose sheetrock does not indicate a structural problem, it is annoying and should not have to be tolerated.

Cracks in the sheetrock, however, can mean structural abnormalities. For example, there may be a settlement problem. If just one room has been refinished, find out why. Did an upstairs tub overflow? Did the roof leak? Was the damage patched or totally repaired? Is something being hidden?

PLASTER

Plaster walls and ceilings usually are found in older homes only. It is reasonable to expect the plaster to have cracks. However, they should be small; hairline and hardly noticeable. Plaster holes or cracks are not as easy to fix as those in sheetrock. When plaster is patched or repaired, it has a tendency to crack in the same place at a later date. Check plaster walls and ceilings carefully for deterioration or plaster pulling loose. These problems could indicate the need for major repair and perhaps total replacement of the plaster walls. Problems of deterioration are more likely to occur in areas with high moisture content or in a house that has been vacant for an extended period.

CEILINGS

Ceilings typically have a smooth painted finish, but there are several alternatives. One is a stippled or textured ceiling. These ceilings have the sheetrock compound rolled, brushed, or sprayed on in a particular pattern. Some of these patterns are swirled, others are randomly blotched. Sometimes this same method is used to finish walls.

Although the sheetrock ceiling is by far the most common, the drop ceiling is also popular. The drop ceiling is installed with a metal grid system and ceiling tile panels. These panels should be level. Damaged tiles can be replaced, if the same design panels are available. However, age often discolors the tiles and the new ones do not match. If you can't get the kind of faithful match your aesthetic taste demands, you may have to replace the entire ceiling. Water stains are quite obvious in drop ceilings. Sometimes they are caused by leaks from the flashing of the roof, siding or windows. Another cause could be leaky water or drain lines. Ask about the cause behind any water stains.

Ceilings may droop for the same reason that walls bow. Using wood with an excessive crown will never give good results. If the ceiling does droop or appear to roll, you may have a problem that will be quite expensive to correct. When the ceiling in one room has a problem, you are likely to find that problem repeated in other rooms. If sheetrock tape shows at the junction of the ceiling and the wall, the sheetrock compound was not applied properly. Often the cause of weak tape seams is the application of a watered down compound. That kind of diluted compound is acceptable for stippling and texturing, but too thin for sheetrock finishing.

Sometimes the seam is cut when wallpaper is being applied. This can happen when the paper is razor trimmed against the wall. The razor blade cuts through the tape because the tape did not have enough compound. If the cut is very noticeable it can be corrected by retaping, recompounding, repainting, or repapering. If the flaw is a small one, such a repair is hardly worth the effort.

Checklist #5: Roofing, Insulation, and Interior Walls

	House #1 Location:_____	NO PROBLEM	MINIMUM	MINOR	MAJOR	HOLD
		0	1	2	3	?
1	Do you see any color changes in the roofing?					
2	Does the roof have a guarantee?					
3	What are the specifics of the roof guarantee? Proration?					
4	Is the roof turning up at the edges, cracking or blistering?					
5	Cedar shakes: Are any shakes deteriorating?					
6	Can you see any felt through the roofing?					
7	Will you need to remove the existing roofing before reroofing?					
8	Skylights: Have there been any problems with leaks?					
9	Does the house have formaldehyde insulation? Family allergies?					
10	Does the house have good quality wall and ceiling insulation?					
11	Does the house have proper roof ventilation?					
12	Crawl space: Does it have foundation vents?					
13	Will the energy bills fit your budget?					
14	Do the interior walls have any major defects?					
15	Do the walls have any unsightly bows?					
16	Is all sheetrock secured?					
17	Are there any cracks in the sheetrock? Warning: May be structural.					
18	Plaster walls: Do they need repair?					
19	Drop ceiling: Will any tiles need replacing?					
20	Drop ceiling: Do you see any water stains?					
21	Do any ceilings droop or appear to roll?					
22	Can you see any exposed sheetrock tape?					
23	Any problems with Radon gas in the area?					
24	REMARKS OR OTHER:					
25						
26						
27						
28						
29						
30						

TRANSFER SUB-TOTALS TO
MASTER CHECKLIST FORM

SUB-TOTAL				

ADDITIONAL REMARKS OR OTHERS:

Checklist #5: Roofing, Insulation, and Interior Walls

	House #2 Location:_____	NO PROBLEM	MINIMUM	MINOR	MAJOR	HOLD
		0	1	2	3	?
1	Do you see any color changes in the roofing?					
2	Does the roof have a guarantee?					
3	What are the specifics of the roof guarantee? Proration?					
4	Is the roof turning up at the edges, cracking or blistering?					
5	Cedar shakes: Are any shakes deteriorating?					
6	Can you see any felt through the roofing?					
7	Will you need to remove the existing roofing before reroofing?					
8	Skylights: Have there been any problems with leaks?					
9	Does the house have formaldehyde insulation? Family allergies?					
10	Does the house have good quality wall and ceiling insulation?					
11	Does the house have proper roof ventilation?					
12	Crawl space: Does it have foundation vents?					
13	Will the energy bills fit your budget?					
14	Do the interior walls have any major defects?					
15	Do the walls have any unsightly bows?					
16	Is all sheetrock secured?					
17	Are there any cracks in the sheetrock? Warning: May be structural.					
18	Plaster walls: Do they need repair?					
19	Drop ceiling: Will any tiles need replacing?					
20	Drop ceiling: Do you see any water stains?					
21	Do any ceilings droop or appear to roll?					
22	Can you see any exposed sheetrock tape?					
23	Any problems with Radon gas in the area?					
24	REMARKS OR OTHER:					
25						
26						
27						
28						
29						
30						

TRANSFER SUB-TOTALS TO
MASTER CHECKLIST FORM

| SUB-TOTAL | | | | |

ADDITIONAL REMARKS OR OTHERS:

_____

_____

_____

_____

_____

_____

_____

_____

_____

_____

_____

_____

_____

Checklist #5: Roofing, Insulation, and Interior Walls

		NO PROBLEM	MINIMUM	MINOR	MAJOR	HOLD
	House #3 Location:_____					
		0	1	2	3	?
1	Do you see any color changes in the roofing?					
2	Does the roof have a guarantee?					
3	What are the specifics of the roof guarantee? Proration?					
4	Is the roof turning up at the edges, cracking or blistering?					
5	Cedar shakes: Are any shakes deteriorating?					
6	Can you see any felt through the roofing?					
7	Will you need to remove the existing roofing before reroofing?					
8	Skylights: Have there been any problems with leaks?					
9	Does the house have formaldehyde insulation? Family allergies?					
10	Does the house have good quality wall and ceiling insulation?					
11	Does the house have proper roof ventilation?					
12	Crawl space: Does it have foundation vents?					
13	Will the energy bills fit your budget?					
14	Do the interior walls have any major defects?					
15	Do the walls have any unsightly bows?					
16	Is all sheetrock secured?					
17	Are there any cracks in the sheetrock? Warning: May be structural.					
18	Plaster walls: Do they need repair?					
19	Drop ceiling: Will any tiles need replacing?					
20	Drop ceiling: Do you see any water stains?					
21	Do any ceilings droop or appear to roll?					
22	Can you see any exposed sheetrock tape?					
23	Any problems with Radon gas in the area?					
24	REMARKS OR OTHER:					
25						
26						
27						
28						
29						
30						
	SUB-TOTAL					

TRANSFER SUB-TOTALS TO
MASTER CHECKLIST FORM

ADDITIONAL REMARKS OR OTHERS:

6: Interior Trim, Paint, and Floors

Chapter six focuses on some of the items that begin to give the house its personality; those embellishments that reflect the owner's (or the builder's) personal taste. If you buy the house before its construction has been completed, you will have the opportunity to impose your own taste. There are choices to be made concerning cabinet design, door style, trim, etc. The addition of "personally selected" windows, doors, cabinets, molding, and so on, begins to give the house a look, a personality that will be pleasing to the owner.

If you are looking at a previously occupied house, ask yourself questions. Do I like the overall style? Is it too modern when my preference is colonial style? Do the wallpaper and floor coverings please me? Will I want to replace more items (or do more items need replacing?) than I want to keep? These are important questions to consider, as you ponder what might be substantial "after closing" costs.

INTERIOR TRIM
The list of interior trim items is a long one, comprised of:
- interior doors and locks
- windows and window locks
- cabinets and vanities
- step railings
- paneling
- closet accessories
- floor coverings
- all types of molding.

PANELING
Wall paneling is offered in many styles, colors, and sizes, made of almost any wood product. Sheet paneling is the most common type. It customarily is prefinished and put in place with matching nails. Sometimes sheet paneling is both glued and nailed. Paneling thickness is important; if it is too thin, it will bow between the framing studs. If thin paneling is used, it should be applied over sheetrock so that this bowing does not occur.

Most paneling is laminated; i.e., a thin sheet of more expensive wood is laminated (glued) to a sheet of less expensive wood or compressed backboard, like Masonite. Some of these compressed boards will take on moisture and swell. Once the wood becomes warped in that way, the problem is impossible to correct. Extra supports between framing studs, called pearlings, are used to prevent paneling from warping. Paneling should be level and plumb.

Nails should be set in unfinished paneling. Setting a nail means that the head is "set" below the level of the paneling so that no unsightly heads protrude. After the nails are set, the baseboard and crown moldings are placed at the floor and ceiling. These trim moldings cover the rough edges of the paneling. Baseboard molding is similarly used to cover the rough edges of a sheetrock wall.

MOLDING
Other moldings usually have names that indicate

their use. Crown molding is installed at the top of the wall. Picture molding resembles the molding you see on a picture frame. Shoe mold is applied at the junction of the wall and the floor. Each of the these moldings comes in different sizes and in many variations. Moldings are made from many different types and grades of wood. Closet rods are made from round moulding that usually is supported, so the weight of the clothing does not cause it to sag.

WINDOW AND DOOR CASINGS

Casings are used to cover up the rough edges of window and door inserts. Usually molding two to three inches wide surrounds the window. Window and door casings do not vary in design and appearance as much as other, more decorative moldings do. Usually they are noticed only if the workmanship (or lack of same) calls attention to them.

Door and window casings are cut on 45 degree angles to match at the corners. When this cut is made improperly, the mismatch is painfully noticeable. Casing nails should be set correctly and no hammer marks should be seen. If the nails have not been properly set, they will work themselves out and protrude.

Remember to check all the locks. They all should operate properly, or the owner should be asked to have them repaired. Some doors are trimmed at the bottom to allow them to open and close smoothly over carpet. If the door bottom looks amateurishly trimmed, you have the right to ask for a replacement.

RAILING AND BRACING

Normally, a run of three steps or more needs a railing. But be aware that a poorly braced railing, giving a false sense of security, can be more dangerous than no railing at all. All railings should be properly braced. A railing braced only to a sheetrock wall is not adequately secured. Nails or screws that penetrate the drywall into a stud will provide good support. In addition to providing support in stairwells, railings also provide security around balconies and decks. Railings usually are wood, but sometimes decorative wrought iron is used (often on a front porch). If small children will be playing in an area enclosed by a railing, pickets can be placed between the vertical rails to ensure no child will fall through and be injured.

CABINETS AND VANITIES

Most new or recently constructed homes have factory-made kitchen cabinets and bathroom vanities. These typically are well-made, with attractive, baked-on finishes. Custom cabinet makers are still in business in some areas, but their numbers are diminishing... and their costs escalating. Still, today's mass-produced cabinets offer a number of "customizing" features, such as lazy Susans, wine racks, and drawers behind doors.

Cabinets and vanities are made from many types and grades of wood and in many different designs and styles. Usually their names will denote the style. "Country Oak" or "Mahogany" may have appearances that match their names, but most of the time they are made of less expensive wood, with veneers or stains that simulate oak or mahogany.

When you examine cabinets and vanities, look for cracks where the wall meets the cabinet. In the warm, frequently humid, environment of a kitchen or bathroom, even a small crack can be a fertile breeding ground for cockroaches. Unattractive and potentially unsanitary, cracks also are places where water can accumulate and begin to corrode the wood, causing it to swell and buckle. The only cure for a countertop that is swollen or buckled is replacement. The problem can only worsen over time. Counter tops are almost always made of plastic laminated to compressed board (Formica is the most widely recognized brand). Once the compressed board is swollen it is beyond repair. If the counter-top has colors that don't quite match, it's likely one section has been replaced.

It is unusual to discover cabinets and vanities that have not been secured properly. If you have any doubt, try a short test. While you open and close the doors, listen and feel for any vibrations. Secured cabinets should feel solid, with no vibrations. If you detect some instability, a well-placed screw or two should solve the problem.

If you are looking at an older home, you may find the kitchen cabinets are structurally sound, but the doors are worn and unattractive. Many homeowners (and homebuyers) are correcting this problem (essentially a cosmetic one) by investing in cabinet "facelifts"; that is, replacing the doors only. It is a compromise solution that seems to satisfy many, and the cost is considerably less than new cabinets.

PAINT

If you have never enjoyed the pleasures of interior housepainting, you might have a less than realistic understanding of what is involved. You don't just buy a brush or roller and a gallon of paint and go to work. While painting is not an exercise in quantum physics, it is more complicated than that. There are paints for interior and exterior walls, metal and concrete, wood and sheetrock. When the incorrect paint is used, the results tend to be less than satisfactory. Even the right paint applied in the wrong way will produce displeasing results. For example, an interior wall that has been spray painted should not be touched up with a brush. The retouched spot will look different, no matter how adroitly the brush work is done. A spray gun creates a different texture. Perhaps you have seen walls that were painted with a roller, then retouched with a brush. The colors may match, but the texture does not.

It is difficult to match paint colors when more than one can is used, even when the same brand/color is purchased. Somehow there always seems to be a very slight difference. When you can, buy all the paint you anticipate you will need at one time, selecting cans with identical batch numbers. Batch numbers add another measure of reliability to color matching. Batches should always match. If you should end up with more paint than was needed, most retailers will refund your money for unopened cans.

INTERIOR PAINT

Examining the paint on the inside of the house may give you more information than you might have expected. Any repainted area within a room will look different from the rest of the room. A shiny or dull spot — anything that looks different — may indicate that something was repaired or covered up. Perhaps an electrical fire around an outlet or switchplate, or a hole patched in sheetrock. If only one part of the house or room has been newly painted, ask the owner why. When only one room in a house has been re-painted, it may only reflect the fact that this particular room is the most used in the house, or it could indicate that a problem occurred in that room. Any time a cosmetic improvement has been made anywhere in the house, it is important to ask questions. You need to know if the damage was completely fixed or if, possibly, the apparent "fix" conceals a more significant problem.

If you are inspecting a completely finished new house, you should find all the walls either painted or papered, and all the sheetrock and trim nails set, puttied, and painted.

If possible, view the house with the lights turned on, even during daylight hours. Incandescent lighting helps to reveal any flaws. If you are really serious about a house, look at it again during the evening with the lights turned on. Some blemishes that did not show in the daytime, even with the lights on, will become more obvious at night. When the light casts shadows, almost all finishing defects can be seen; not only in the paint, but also in the woodwork and sheetrock.

Interior paints come in varying qualities and you usually get what you pay for. If you have children, a good quality, washable latex is worth the price. Latex does not give off offensive odors. It dries quickly. And it cleans easily.

Usually the builder will leave the leftover paint from the house in a storage area (usually the garage or basement). Even the most careful people make a few scuffs and scratches when they move in. If the builder has been thoughtful, you will have exactly the paints you need for any touch-up.

EXTERIOR PAINT

Although most interior walls are sheetrock and compatible paints are abundantly available, the exterior paint used should be specified for the type of exterior finish to which it will be applied.

Acrylic paints are quite popular today, because they withstand the elements well and they are water soluble, allowing the painter easier cleanup. Oil based paints, once a standard exterior paint, are not used very much today for just the opposite reasons. They take much longer to dry, and cleaning up requires a solvent.

If the house has just been painted, examine the paint job for possible irregularities. The work, including the caulking, should look professional. You should not see any cracks in the caulking, or any loose pieces. At least two coats of paint should have been applied to the siding. Fewer than two coats (three is preferable), and you will be repainting sooner than should be necessary. Look closely at the caulking or

wood putty to see if a problem has been covered up. Any spot or area that looks different probably has been redone. If it is a small patch only, it should not be a matter of concern; small nicks or imperfections can develop anywhere, and they are not uncommon. A large and obvious patch, however, should be questioned, especially in an older house. All knotholes should have been caulked, as should have any cracks in the siding.

All the caulking and putty should be dried and adhering to the siding before the paint is applied. If either the putty or caulking is loose, it is either old or has been improperly applied. In either case, the work needs to be redone. A house exterior needs ample time to dry after a rain before paint, putty, or caulking is applied. Otherwise, the caulking pulls loose and the paint peels or flakes. Correctly applied caulking is not just an aesthetic consideration. When a house is not properly caulked, water can penetrate the siding and cause damage. Periodic recaulking and repainting is very important, to prevent water damage and protect the house. A reasonable time span between exterior paintings is three to five years. However, what is reasonable for one house might not apply to another. The length of time a paint job lasts is affected by weather conditions, the quality of the paint used, and the number of coats applied. The more times the siding is painted, the longer the paint should last before the next repainting.

Some sidings are prefinished at a factory, and applied with matching nails and caulking. Prefinished siding requires repainting and recaulking just as frequently as any other kind of siding.

STAIN

When molding and trim items are ready to be finished, they are either painted or stained. Painting is the easier option for the builder, because the walls and woodwork can get the same treatment. There are paints which cover both walls and woodwork. Stains, however, give a rich, warm look to wood. The range of colors available seems almost endless. You could, for example, select dark mahogany or light pecan and the painter could lighten these stains or mix them to satisfy virtually any look you desired

Wood that is to be stained should be in continuous pieces, not cut every foot or so. Small, cut pieces of wood will look fine when painted, but not when stained. Staining wood is a little more complex than simply applying the stain. More than one step is involved. First the stain is applied. Then it is sealed, sanded, and then sealed again with a harder finish. If the stained wood in a house you are checking feels rough to the touch, the second and third steps may have been skipped to save money. Sometimes the sealer is mixed with the stain and a "one coat process" is used, but this does not produce the same results. The wood is not smooth, nor does the finish look as lustrous. Doors that are stained should be sealed on all edges, to keep moisture from penetrating and causing the doors to warp.

WALLPAPER

If the wall is plumb and square, wallpaper hung correctly will be even at the corners, floor, and ceiling. Properly hung paper will have all the patterns matching at the seams. The best paper hanger cannot compensate for a poor construction job, but a non-patterned wallpaper can help conceal some flaws. Check the wallpaper carefully. If a problem is being camouflaged, satisfy yourself that it is a minor one.

Sometimes wallpaper "just happens" to come loose at the edges. Other times there is a cause, a precipitating factor. It may be a roof leak, which can cause both discoloration of the paper and loosening at the edges. Often the humidity in a bathroom will cause the wallpaper to come loose and/or discolor. Attempting to clean a non-washable wallpaper also

could discolor it. The simple remedy for loose wallpaper is simply gluing it back in place. However, if the cause of the problem is not corrected, the problem itself will persist.

Bathroom wallpaper should be vinyl or vinyl coated. Vinyl forms a barrier to block moisture. The same type paper is also the best choice for the kitchen. Grease and cooking odors can quickly ruin a plain, non-protected paper. Because vinyl papers deny moisture penetration, they are washable — another plus in kitchens, bathrooms, children's bedrooms, etc. Wallpaper is produced in runs, with each run number different from all others. Sometimes the difference between runs is barely noticeable; other times it is very evident. All the wallpaper used in a room should be from the same run and purchased at the same time.

If you are considering an older home you may want to change the wallpaper. When you start to remove it, you may find that part of the wall comes off with the paper. That can happen if the wall was not primed or painted before the paper was applied. Sometimes a steam machine can be helpful in removing old paper. And sometimes the job is so hard, so frustrating, you may want to turn it over to a professional. What may be impossibly difficult for you may be a routine job for him.

FLOOR FINISHES

The material that finishes a floor must be able to take the wear and tear of the traffic in and through that area. Floor covering or finishing is one trim item that warrants an investment in quality. A quality floor covering will last perhaps twice as long as an inexpensive covering. Our home, for example, has had the same carpet for fourteen years. Although it may strain the budget to buy the best in the beginning, doing so will prove to have been a good investment.

Virtually all floor finishes are produced in runs or

batches. If matching floor finishes are not used, variations in the finish are unavoidable. Sometimes a large window can affect the appearance of the floor covering because the sun bleaches the area. When you see a variation, ask the owner why the flooring is different. There are innumerable reasons for carpet variations. Sometimes a commode overflows and ruins the flooring. Other times the kids' carpet wears out early and is replaced. Or what strikes you as an unusual variation may merely reflect the owners' taste. A different color in each room was their personal preference.

CARPET

The quality or grade of a carpet is normally determined by the weight of the material used and type of construction. A heavier carpet will have more densely arranged fibers; therefore the weight per measurement is increased. The weight of a carpet is determined by the closeness and length of the fibers.

Although some carpets are blends, carpets usually are made from either nylon or wool. Nylon is the most commonly used material. Some carpet comes with a rubber-type backing. Carpet of this kind usually is glued to the floor, and is used primarily for commercial buildings. It also is useful in the home, over concrete floors in basements and converted garages.

The quality of the padding laid beneath the carpet is almost as important as the quality of the carpet itself. Even an inexpensive carpet will last longer over a good quality padding. Padding is offered in a variety of types and thicknesses. It gives the carpet a soft, spongy bounce while it absorbs the friction produced by human traffic. The better the padding, the more friction-absorbing quality, and the longer the carpet will last.

Carpet wears from the underside as well as from the top. If the carpet is loose and rubs against the pad-

ding, the underside begins to wear and loosen the fibers from underneath. Eventually the fibers will wear loose. When you examine the carpet, look for worn spots. If there are badly worn spots, you probably will want to replace the carpet completely (or ask the owner to do so). You will see some carpeting that is so dirty that its quality and degree of wear are concealed. Cleaning a cheap carpet will only give you a clean, cheap carpet.

If you are buying a new house, you want the carpet to be tightly stretched, with no slack or looseness. Any looseness will cause the carpet to wear much faster. If you see a looseness problem, you can ask the builder to have the carpet restretched.

The weave or nap of the carpet should be going in the same direction throughout the house. Naps that are not matched will exhibit color differences even if all the pieces are from the same batch or run. Brush your hand against the carpet to test the nap. The appearance of these brush marks should be the same in all areas. Since most carpet comes in twelve foot widths, sometimes it must be matched at the seams. If the matching is done properly, the seam is hardly noticeable. If the seam is conspicuous, you can ask to have it redone.

INLAID VINYL

Inlaid vinyl is the most commonly used kitchen floor covering today. Still referred to in some areas as linoleum, vinyl flooring is also being used in bathrooms and foyers. If you notice a problem with a vinyl floor, it probably is the result of poor installation. Inlaid vinyl is glued to the subflooring, but this flooring must first be clear of any defects or blemishes. Any uneven areas must be filled, then sanded; any bumps or hollows that remain will still be visible after the vinyl is installed. If the preliminary work was not done properly, the only possible correction after the vinyl has been installed is total replacement of the flooring.

If possible, the flooring should be laid down in one sheet. Sometimes in a large room, however, a seam is inevitable. Problems naturally gravitate toward seams. The causes can be poor installation, but even normal mopping over a seam will loosen it eventually. Whether seamed or not, the pattern of the inlaid should match evenly at all edges of the floors. When the pattern is not matched, it means that the installer was careless. In a "worst case" scenario, it could mean that the room is out of square. If the poor matching is an installation problem, a new floor will correct it. If the room is out of square, you could redo the floor with a non-patterned vinyl... or you may decide to make your house investment elsewhere.

High and low places also can indicate construction problems (the crown of a floor joist, for example). If the area is over a crawl space, the problem may be corrected by cutting and adding another floor joist from underneath. When the floor squeaks, the cause may be the sub-floor. In order to fix the sub-flooring, however, you will have to destroy the inlaid vinyl, then replace it.

High or low spots in a concrete floor certainly will affect the smoothness of vinyl flooring. The problem can be corrected (and the flooring replaced), but it is an expensive repair. If the concrete was not leveled after it was poured, you might not want to attempt it now depending on the severity of the problem. You probably will choose to either live with the problem or walk away from it.

VINYL TILE

Vinyl tile also is a popular floor covering for kitchens, baths, and foyers. These tiles are available in squares (or other shapes), a foot square or smaller. Tiles either have an independent pattern, or one that is part of an overall pattern, that needs to be matched to adjacent tiles. Tiles also come in solid colors.

Inlaid tiles offer one advantage over inlaid vinyl.

A damaged area can be corrected by the removal of individual tiles. This repair/replacement work requires some skill, because the damaged tiles must be heated in order to remove them. Small bumps and problems could possibly be corrected this way. If you are going to attempt to make this repair yourself, check first to make sure that matching tiles are available. If they are not, you could find yourself replacing the entire floor. Any cracked, curled, or loose tiles are potential safety hazards, and should be replaced.

CERAMIC TILE

Ceramic tile has been a flooring alternative for a long time. It also has been popular in the kitchen for walls and counter tops as well. Perhaps the biggest drawback of ceramic tile is cost. Partly handmade and usually imported, they can help give a house a distinctive look. However, you do pay a premium for this individuality. In today's market, ceramic tile is typically two to three times the price of vinyl flooring.

In many older houses, not only are the floors ceramic, so are the walls, the towel holders, the soap dish, etc. If any of these holders were not put in place securely, they could work loose over time. When that happens, remove it, add blocking for backing and reinstall the old fixture (or replace it with a new one). When floor or wall tiles are loose, you should suspect water damage and investigate the cause. Water damage can also cause the grout to crack or come loose. If water damage is the problem, you will have to take up the old tile and correct whatever is causing the damage. Sometimes you can reuse the tiles, but usually it is more practical to replace the entire floor or wall.

When one tile is cracked, it is possible to replace it if other tile is still available with the same batch number. If several tiles are cracked, you may be looking at a structural problem (or it could be the result of a household accident). If the cracks are the result of house settlement, you could be looking at a serious structural problem. You may not know if the problem has resolved itself (i.e., the settling has stopped) or whether the condition will worsen. This is another case where the prudent buyer asks the owner what happened.

WOOD FLOORS

Most houses constructed before 1970 have wood flooring. Today wood floors in medium priced houses are rare. Wood floors should be installed by skilled professionals, and that ability has its price.

There are, basically, two kinds of wood flooring. One, glued to the floor in pieces, is known as parquet flooring. While parquet flooring is square, glued wooden flooring also comes in small strips. This kind of wood flooring normally is prefinished; once it is glued it is ready for a sealant. When you examine a parquet floor, step on several pieces at random to see if they are securely in place. If you have just one or two loose pieces, you can secure them with thin finishing nails. You then set each nail and fill each small nail hole with putty that is colored to match the wood flooring.

"Basketball court" wood flooring is the other basic type. It is like the old oak flooring that fits together with a tongue and groove. The pieces are then nailed in place, "toenailed" so the nails do not show. After the floor is installed, it is sanded, stained (optional), and varnished. This flooring can be resanded and refinished when it begins to show signs of wear.

Both types of wood flooring are available in various types, grades, and sizes. If you consider replacing wood flooring in an older house, check that matching replacements are available. Even when the replacement flooring is available, it may not match an existing floor which has aged.

When you examine wood floors, you will be looking for continuity. Any putty between floorboards is there to fill gaps caused by shrinkage. This shrinkage may continue. Ask the owner when the putty was applied. If some time has passed since that was done, perhaps the shrinkage has stabilized. Houses in areas with considerable temperature and moisture fluctuations are apt to have more wood floor problems than those in other parts of the country.

BRICK/SLATE/MOSAIC TILE/MARBLE

Brick, slate, and mosaic tile are beautiful flooring materials. When installed properly, they endure attractively for the life of the house — and beyond. (Many old houses have been razed, with the brick, slate, or tile floors still intact, still usable). Brick and slate are normally imbedded in a cement base. When the base is dry, the joints are grouted. The installation of mosaic tile and marble floors is basically the same as that of ceramic tile floors.

When you examine these floors, you want to find all the pieces intact and the floor surface entirely level. Loose pieces are a safety hazard, and an uneven floor will make any furniture unsteady. Cracks in the floors could mean structural damage. If a piece sounds hollow when you walk across the floor, it was improperly installed. It probably was not imbedded deeply enough to make a solid connection. The resulting air space causes the hollow sound.

Any loose grout should be replaced. High or low spots, in either brick, slate, or mosaic tile, can create a safety hazard. Anyone walking across the floor could trip on the uneven piece. If the surface of the floor is very smooth, you also could have a safety hazard. Water spots also are hazardous, especially with mosaic tile. Although mosaic tile and marble create beautiful floors, they are very slippery when wet. Extreme caution should be used when coming in from the rain or in any other situations that might leave water droplets on the floor.

Checklist #6: Interior Trim, Paint, and Floors

	House #1 Location:_____	NO PROBLEM	MINIMUM	MINOR	MAJOR	HOLD
		0	1	2	3	?
1	Paneling: Does it bow between the framing studs?					
2	Paneling: Is it warped?					
3	Paneling: Are all the nails "set"?					
4	Do all the doors and windows open and close without difficulty?					
5	Are the door and window locks working properly?					
6	Railings: Are they secured and braced?					
7	Did you find any problems with the kitchen cabinets?					
8	Will you need to consider a kitchen cabinet facelift?					
9	Has there been any water damage to the kitchen/bath countertops?					
10	Does the outside of the house need repainting?					
11	Is the outside caulking in good condition?					
12	Do you think any interior paint is hiding a problem?					
13	Are the walls properly nailed, puttied and painted?					
14	Are you pleased with the woodwork, moldings, etc.?					
15	Did you see any problems with the wallpaper?					
16	Will you change some of the wallpaper?					
17	Are the carpets in good condition? Replacement soon?					
18	New House: Can you afford an upgrade in carpet?					
19	Is the carpet stretched sufficiently?					
20	Are there any bumps in the vinyl flooring?					
21	Will you need to repair any flooring?					
22	Ceramic Tile: Any cracked or broken pieces to repair?					
23	Ceramic Tile Bathrooms: Are all tiles secure? Fixtures, too?					
24	Do you see any water damage in the bathrooms?					
25	Wooden Floors: Are they finished and sealed correctly? Splinters?					
26	Wooden Floors: Will they need to be refinished?					
27	Misc. Flooring: Is the grout coming up? Repairs needed?					
28	REMARKS OR OTHER:					
29						
30						
	SUB-TOTAL					

TRANSFER SUB-TOTALS TO
MASTER CHECKLIST FORM

ADDITIONAL REMARKS OR OTHERS:

_____

_____

_____

_____

_____

_____

_____

_____

_____

_____

_____

_____

_____

Checklist #6: Interior Trim, Paint, and Floors

	House #2 Location:_____	NO PROBLEM	MINIMUM	MINOR	MAJOR	HOLD
		0	1	2	3	?
1	Paneling: Does it bow between the framing studs?					
2	Paneling: Is it warped?					
3	Paneling: Are all the nails "set"?					
4	Do all the doors and windows open and close without difficulty?					
5	Are the door and window locks working properly?					
6	Railings: Are they secured and braced?					
7	Did you find any problems with the kitchen cabinets?					
8	Will you need to consider a kitchen cabinet facelift?					
9	Has there been any water damage to the kitchen/bath countertops?					
10	Does the outside of the house need repainting?					
11	Is the outside caulking in good condition?					
12	Do you think any interior paint is hiding a problem?					
13	Are the walls properly nailed, puttied and painted?					
14	Are you pleased with the woodwork, moldings, etc.?					
15	Did you see any problems with the wallpaper?					
16	Will you change some of the wallpaper?					
17	Are the carpets in good condition? Replacement soon?					
18	New House: Can you afford an upgrade in carpet?					
19	Is the carpet stretched sufficiently?					
20	Are there any bumps in the vinyl flooring?					
21	Will you need to repair any flooring?					
22	Ceramic Tile: Any cracked or broken pieces to repair?					
23	Ceramic Tile Bathrooms: Are all tiles secure? Fixtures, too?					
24	Do you see any water damage in the bathrooms?					
25	Wooden Floors: Are they finished and sealed correctly? Splinters?					
26	Wooden Floors: Will they need to be refinished?					
27	Misc. Flooring: Is the grout coming up? Repairs needed?					
28	REMARKS OR OTHER:					
29						
30						
	SUB-TOTAL					

TRANSFER SUB-TOTALS TO
MASTER CHECKLIST FORM

ADDITIONAL REMARKS OR OTHERS:

_____

_____

_____

_____

_____

_____

_____

_____

_____

_____

_____

_____

_____

_____

_____

_____

_____

Checklist #6: Interior Trim, Paint, and Floors

	House #3 Location:_____	NO PROBLEM 0	MINIMUM 1	MINOR 2	MAJOR 3	HOLD ?
1	Paneling: Does it bow between the framing studs?					
2	Paneling: Is it warped?					
3	Paneling: Are all the nails "set"?					
4	Do all the doors and windows open and close without difficulty?					
5	Are the door and window locks working properly?					
6	Railings: Are they secured and braced?					
7	Did you find any problems with the kitchen cabinets?					
8	Will you need to consider a kitchen cabinet facelift?					
9	Has there been any water damage to the kitchen/bath countertops?					
10	Does the outside of the house need repainting?					
11	Is the outside caulking in good condition?					
12	Do you think any interior paint is hiding a problem?					
13	Are the walls properly nailed, puttied and painted?					
14	Are you pleased with the woodwork, moldings, etc.?					
15	Did you see any problems with the wallpaper?					
16	Will you change some of the wallpaper?					
17	Are the carpets in good condition? Replacement soon?					
18	New House: Can you afford an upgrade in carpet?					
19	Is the carpet stretched sufficiently?					
20	Are there any bumps in the vinyl flooring?					
21	Will you need to repair any flooring?					
22	Ceramic Tile: Any cracked or broken pieces to repair?					
23	Ceramic Tile Bathrooms: Are all tiles secure? Fixtures, too?					
24	Do you see any water damage in the bathrooms?					
25	Wooden Floors: Are they finished and sealed correctly? Splinters?					
26	Wooden Floors: Will they need to be refinished?					
27	Misc. Flooring: Is the grout coming up? Repairs needed?					
28	REMARKS OR OTHER:					
29						
30						
	SUB-TOTAL					

TRANSFER SUB-TOTALS TO
MASTER CHECKLIST FORM

ADDITIONAL REMARKS OR OTHERS:

_____

_____

_____

_____

_____

_____

_____

_____

_____

_____

_____

_____

_____

7: Built-in Appliances and Interior/Exterior Amenities

Information in this chapter will help you focus first on the kitchen (and maybe the laundry room), and the various built-in appliances there, then on a variety of outside amenities.

Although ovens, surface units, microwaves, and other kitchen appliances are considered necessities, they differ so in quality and range of features that you should examine them in the light of those considerations. A "top of the line" assortment of kitchen appliances, for example, may be worth thousands of dollars more than "economy" appliances. If you are comparing two previously owned, structurally identical houses, and the owners of those houses have made different purchase and selection decisions throughout each house — one "top of the line", the other "economy" — the cost of the "top of the line" house may exceed the cost of the "economy" house by $10,000 or more. Is the additional value worth the additional cost? That's up to you.

For example . . . is a Jenn-Air surface unit worth the premium — to you — over a national chain's standard model? Is it important to you that the clothes dryer has seven drying cycles and more bells and whistles than a steam calliope? There aren't any generalized right or wrong answers to such questions as these; only answers that are right or wrong for you. And there is no inference to be drawn here that any chain or national brand's standard models are poor quality. Virtually all of them give you what you pay for. It all depends on what you want, and what you are prepared/willing to pay. You can get from here to there in a Mercedes . . . or a Ford Escort . . . even a Yugo.

Looking at the appliances in a new home is different. The equipment will be under warranty, and the cost of replacements will not be a consideration in the near future. In older homes, however, you will want to ask questions about the age and efficiency of the appliances. Any owner should be willing to answer your questions.

BUILT-INS

The function of this book is to help you inspect, evaluate, and rate residential properties, both new and previously occupied. It will not attempt to be a consumer's guide to new appliances. You expect them to work. If they do not, you have your warranties as insurance. Nevertheless, know what you want in and expect from a kitchen. So much family time is spent there, it should contain just about all the space, equipment, and features you want. You don't want to be thinking (after you have moved in), "I wish I had insisted on . . ." every time you walk in the kitchen.

When you are looking at used equipment, turn the knobs and open the doors. Does the oven timer still work? If a burner is defective, can you get a replacement? Does the refrigerator's automatic defrost still work . . . automatically?

If a major appliance needs replacement, finding one of the same size to fill the space available may not be easy. There are many kitchen appliance brands, and some of the manufacturers are no longer in business. If the built-in oven needs to be replaced, can you find a new one of the same dimensions, so you don't have to rework the cabinets or walls? Measure the opening size and call the supplier of the old oven to find out if a "fitting" replacement is available. If the same size is not obtainable, the original brand or any other, you would have to redo the cabinet opening(s), a potentially expensive proposition.

SURFACE UNIT/OVEN/RANGE/ RANGE HOOD

A surface unit is a cooking top, separate from the oven, that fits into an open space in the counter top. There are gas and electric surface units. Some gas units have a pilot light, others have electric ignition. Some older gas units have neither, however, so a match has to be struck each time the surface unit is used. The electric ignition is the safest; a pilot light next. There are many kinds of gas and electric surface units, with a variety of options and features that affect the price. When you examine any kitchen equipment, turn on all the switches, burners, etc. to ensure that each unit is in working order.

One potential hazard to check is the proximity of the cooking top burners to the wall. Do the walls next to the surface unit look scorched? If so, that indicates that the burners are too close. While this is not a common problem, it is a true safety hazard; there is a greater likelihood that an unattended or forgotten pot, or perhaps a small grease

fire, will ignite the wall. The correction for this problem is major cabinet reconstruction.

If the kitchen has a free-standing or built-in stove (surface cooktop and oven in one unit), you will want to conduct the same kind of inspection; i.e., turn on the oven(s) to see that it works properly and check to determine that all the buttons and/or settings for each burner function as they should.

Microwave ovens can be built-in or set on the counter top. Sometimes they are part of an oven/stove combination. Check the buttons and controls with the same care you do every other appliance.

Range hoods vent kitchen odors and fumes. Some hoods are vented to the outside, others are ductless. The ductpipe should lead to the outside, not the attic. If the duct leads to the attic, a kitchen fire could spread the fire to the attic. A ductless hood has no vent pipe. It vents the air through a charcoal filter and back into the room. Filters of both types should be cleaned regularly to allow for proper ventilation. While you are checking the hood exhaust fan, check the light as well.

DISHWASHER

Dishwashers typically are built into kitchen cabinets, especially in new homes, with free standing units usually found in older homes. When you check out the dishwasher, look for rust, leaks, or evidence of past problems with leaks. Does the seal of the door fit tightly? Dishwashers can be purchased that are energy efficient. These models save on both water and electricity. However, some users of these models have complained that the energy savers don't clean as well as the standard models. If a house you are inspecting has such a unit, ask the owner if she has been satisfied with its performance.

OTHER

There are many other kitchen appliances that can be built into cabinets. Trash compactors, water dispensers, and garbage disposals are the most common. Some "authorities" recommend against connecting a garbage disposal to a septic tank system because of the backup problems it may cause. Other homeowners who have made such a connection report no such problem — if the septic tank is drained regularly (every three-four years).

Check all the appliances that are being sold as part of the overall house purchase. You wouldn't think of buying a used car without at least driving it around the block, trying the radio, heater, windshield wipers, etc. in the process. Look at a house purchase (a much more consequential investment) in the same way. Try out the extras to be sure they work. Ask about any warranties that still may be in effect. If you are going to buy the house, you have a right to know all the facts.

AMENITIES

Some of the built-ins and other special kitchen features are sometimes referred to as amenities. Amenities usually are thought of as tangible items, things you can put your hands on. They can also be "situations" or "feelings". Nice neighborhoods and convenient shopping are amenities. If the house you are looking at is a "member" of a neighborhood association which shares some common property, you should check out that property, all the facilities, as if you were the sole owner. If you find that the condition of these shared facilities is poor, it may mean that the dues are not sufficient to cover the upkeep. If that is the case, dues may soon increase.

SWIMMING POOL

Swimming pools vary in construction, size, and shape. In recent years, long and narrow lap pools have become very popular. Pool costs vary sig-

nificantly, depending on all the variables mentioned. The gunite pool is the standard of the industry and enjoys the widest use. It has steel reinforced sides and bottom, with inside walls made from masonry products. Gunite pools usually are set in the ground.

Certain problems, primarily pitting and cracking of the plaster, are specific to gunite pools. Replastering a gunite pool is not uncommon, because of the effects of time and normal use. If the pH of the water is not maintained correctly, the pool walls will pit. Harsh chemicals also can cause pitting. Examine the pool carefully for cracks and pitting. If these conditions exist, the correction is replastering.

The vinyl-lined pool is the typical above the ground pool. Sometimes it is set half way or all the way in the ground at the deepest end. If the property you are inspecting has this type of pool, examine the liner patches. The liner is subject to tears that require patching; the more patches, the sooner a new liner will be required. If it appears that a new liner will be needed, ask the owner if the company that installed the pool is still in business. If not, an expensive, special order liner might be needed.

Both gunite and vinyl-lined pools have skimmers that keep the surface free of leaves and other debris. Check to see that the skimmers work properly. The entire pool filtering system should be in good order and working efficiently. Faulty equipment leads to breakdowns and replacements.

All pools require chemicals to keep the water safe for swimming. These chemicals are not inexpensive. The greatest cost is incurred at the beginning of the season, when the pool is "opened". The chemical maintenance cost continues through the swimming season. Does the pool appear to have been maintained properly? If the pool is heated, ask the owner how that affects his monthly utility bill during the season. Pools are fun but they require considerable upkeep and almost constant vigilance. It is for good reason that an insurance policy will refer to a pool as an "attractive nuisance". If you have a friend who has a pool, ask for his opinion.

POOL DECKING

Pool decking is the walkway and area immediately surrounding the pool. Wood deckings usually are built around above ground pools, while concrete aprons (sometimes bricked or with another decorative finish) are used around gunite pools. As a safety measure, both the pool and the decking should be fenced. This is required by law in some areas.

Another safety consideration: the decking should not be slippery. Any cracks, usually the result of settling, also can be dangerous and should be repaired. Cracks in concrete decking could mean settlement problems. Settlement cracks in the apron also can affect the pool. Make your inspection very carefully.

FENCING

When people think about fencing, they usually picture a chain link or wooden fence. The chain link fence is the type most commonly used to enclose the entire backyard. It is effective for keeping small children safely contained, and the best fencing for animals because it is "bite-proof", and generally unbreakable. However, dogs (and some industrious children) have been known to tunnel under chain link fences.

Wooden fences provide privacy, and they are cosmetically more appealing. When a family wants a buffer from the street, they usually choose a wooden fence. Although wooden fencing is much more attractive than metal, it does

impose maintenance requirements and it has a shorter life span. Once the chain link fence is in place, you can forget about it. However, like the siding of the house, a wood fence will have to be painted or sealed periodically.

When you examine fencing, look for any missing parts. Do the gates open and close without difficulty? If it is a wooden fence, will it need painting soon? Has the fence been well maintained? Does the gate have a working lock? The owner may not be interested in repairing a rotted or unsightly wooden fence, but you can ask for a compensating reduction in price.

FIREPLACE

Basically there are two types of fireplace. The masonry fireplace has been built "from scratch", usually when the house was constructed. The second type is prebuilt, with a metal firebox and metal chase. Most people prefer the masonry fireplace, but a prebuilt unit is a cost effective alternative.

The masonry fireplace requires a footing. The size and style can be whatever the builder or buyer desires. Because they are designed to take on the extra temperature, wood stoves can be safely inserted into masonry fireplaces. However, you would be prudent to check with the manufacturer of a prebuilt fireplace before attempting to insert a wood burning stove.

The draft of a fireplace is very important. When you examine the fireplace, light a match and place it inside (making sure the damper is open). Does the smoke draft up the chase? Check a prebuilt fireplace the same way.

Although prebuilt fireplaces can be cost effective, they are often used for their appearance rather than their heating ability. If the prebuilt is to be a good heating source, it must have a pipe to the outside for air. This pipe is called an outside combustion air vent. The fireplace needs to burn oxygen from a source other than house air. A metal framed, glass fireplace screen is very useful, because it lessens the draft of the fireplace and allows heat to radiate back into the house. Prebuilt fireplaces come in a variety of sizes, with inside facing of rock, stone, or brick.

Either fireplace may have a gas starter to help the fire to build faster. Improperly installed gas starters can leak and allow gas to build up in the fireplace or chase. Ask the owner about the gas starter and any problems that might have occurred. A properly installed, efficiently operating gas starter is a useful device, because it cuts the starting time in half.

The roof line also is important to either type fireplace. The chimney should be at least two feet higher than the roof peak. This is a safety factor which allows the fireplace to draft properly and keep the smoke from drafting back into the house. When you are inside the house, look around the fireplace. Do you see any smoke damage? Any fire damage? Either might be an indication that the fireplace does not draft properly. The damage also could have been the result of a larger fire being built than the fireplace was designed to handle. If a fire is started with the damper closed, the smoke will bellow into the house. This could be the cause of some smoke stains.

All fireplace chases should be cleaned out at least once a year, either before or after seasonal use. It is a good idea to also clean out the chase midway through the cold season. If you see other signs of inadequate fireplace maintenance, ask when the chase was last cleaned.

When you are about to make any major investment, and a house certainly is in that category, there is no such thing as a dumb question. If you are uncertain about anything, ask — especially in circumstances where evidence points toward a previous mishap. Fireplaces have flashing around the chimney at the roof. Flashing often leaks. Look at the ceiling at the junction of the fireplace. Do you see any water stains or damage? If so, it's likely the flashing needs repair or replacement. Flashing that has leaked also may have affected the surrounding wood, causing damage which also requires repair.

A wood burning stove is best for someone who is really serious about reducing heating cost. There are certain restrictions that must be followed in the use of a wood stove, or a serious fire could result. Wood stoves can burn at six hundred plus degrees. Temperatures that high can ignite surrounding furnishings, draperies, etc. The manufacturers of wood stoves, therefore, have precise instructions and recommendations that should be strictly followed. The most strict warnings concern distances between the stove and its surroundings. Sometimes surrounding areas must be covered with fire brick. Your interest in a wood stove will depend on how serious you are about reducing your energy bill. A wood stove can really help, but the safety responsibilities that go with it should be carefully considered.

HOT TUBS, SAUNAS, ETC.
Hot tubs, whirlpools, and saunas, like swimming pools, have equipment upkeep and maintenance requirements to accompany the pleasures they bring. The hot tub and whirlpool require chemicals to keep the water safe, and sometimes they are afflicted with equipment problems. If there is a problem, is the pump accessible or would you have a hard time getting to it? Is the equipment in good condition ? How old is the unit ? How much time per week is usually needed for maintenance? The bottom line question: Would the pleasures you derive more than offset the responsibilities you would incur? If not, you may regret having paid a premium for what you thought of as a luxury appliance, but what is actually — for you — an "attractive nuisance".

SECURITY SYSTEMS

There are two basic kinds of security systems. One just sets the alarm off in the house, while the other also alerts some outside authority. Will the security system work when the power is off? Is there a backup, battery-powered system? If the system is to be truly effective all outside window and door openings should be connected to it. Remember to "take it for a test drive"; in other words, test the system to see how well it works.

OTHER AMENITIES

It is almost impossible to identify and consider every possible amenity. It is more important for you to know how — and if — each amenity works; if not, who will fix it. If it is in operating condition, do you know how to use it? Do you understand the maintenance requirements? Does it have a warranty?

The next few paragraphs describe some amenities you are less likely to see but should know about just in case. An underground lawn sprinkler system is a fantastic labor saver. However, at the end of each season, you should either flush the pipes with antifreeze or blow them out with air, under pressure, to keep them from bursting (in areas which have freezing temperatures). If the system is on a timer, you will need to understand the workings of the timing system. Careful inspection and test use should tell you if the entire system has been well maintained.

While many people truly enjoy their greenhouses, they are notorious for leaks. It is difficult to keep caulking from contracting and expanding when exposed to the elements. Ask the owner if the caulking has been replaced; and if so, when? Look for any broken glass; it should be replaced by the owner. If the greenhouse does not have an exhaust fan or a heating system, the plants are likely to suffer from temperature extremes. If there is an automatic watering system, have the owner demonstrate it and ask questions about maintenance and upkeep.

Screened porches are lovely. All the screens should be intact or on your "seller's repair" list. Any rotten wood also should be repaired or replaced (or compensation provided). Check the porch very carefully for wood rot. That is a common problem for wood exposed to the elements from all sides.

Some houses have intercom systems which allow voice communication and/or music throughout the house. To test it, turn it on before you tour the house. You will learn, as you go from room to room, whether each speaker is working. The system can be very useful for families with children.

You may find that the intercom system (and perhaps the lighting, environmental controls, security system, etc.) is connected to a household computer, the latest home amenity. Unless the builder or seller is promoting a multi-purpose, computer system as a major reason to buy the house, it is unlikely that a computer would be offered with the house. If the house does have a computer, however (and if it does, you will be paying for it), you, or another family member, will want to understand how to utilize it fully. If you don't have that capability immediately, you at least will want to know where to turn for assistance and service.

Built in household vacuum systems have been around for quite a few years. They don't seem to be as popular as they once were, but you still may come across one — especially in a resale house. Ask the owner if all the outlets work. Do they use the system or is it a nuisance rather than a timesaver? Are replacement parts available? When was the system last serviced?

Automatic timers, useful in curbing energy costs, are available for lights, heating and air conditioning, water heaters, etc. These devices come with specific instructions so be sure that the user manuals are still available. Some water heater energy savers may be unintentionally deceptive. These are water heater timers which heat the water on demand, rather than maintaining a large tank of hot water. If you are using a lot of hot water steadily, all during the day, this device will not be cost efficient; it takes more energy to heat the water quickly, on demand. For this kind of steady usage, a regular hot water heater would be more economical. The timer which works on demand is better suited to the family that leaves the house in the morning and returns in the evening, since the water is not kept hot when there is no one to use it.

Occasionally you will come across a solar water heater. If you do, you will find an energy conscious owner who will tell you all you need to know (probably more) about the system.

If you are fortunate enough to be looking at a house with an automatic sprinkler system for fire control, you will have an added measure of security if you buy the house. Ask the owner the age of the system; it probably will be the same age as the house. Also ask him who services the system and what has to be done to keep it in working order. Has the system ever been used? Have there been any false alarms? If the house has fire extinguishers, the date should be current or the unit replaced. Check the hose on the extinguisher; it cannot deliver the foam if the hose is not in good condition.

Choosing a Builder and/or a Real Estate Agent

If you have read all the pages that precede this section, you know that selecting a house that is right for you and your family — that doesn't have any expensive "time bombs" waiting to explode (after you have moved in) — is a painstaking task. Because it is such an important investment, you want to make the wisest, most informed selection possible. If you have decided to have a house built, you will want to bring the same considerations to bear on your selection of a builder.

You understand now all the elements that make a residential property attractive, from neighborhood to lot to placement of the house on the property to all the details of the house itself. When you choose a builder, you are looking for someone with the knowledge and experience to build the house with professional skill and the integrity to ensure that everything you cannot see is equal in quality to all the elements that are visible.

Because there are so many variables involved, no two houses are exactly alike. Even though many of the basics might be the same — lumber, concrete, plumbing and heating, and electrical service — such finishing items as fixtures, carpets, ceilings, built-ins, and various amenities will give your house its own personality. All of that work has to be done correctly, so the first ingredient you look for in a builder is knowledge of his trade. There are very few schools that instruct in all the aspects of home construction, so experience (often gained through one or more apprenticeships) is still the primary teacher. Honesty is an important virtue, but that probably is the second attribute you look for. The most honest builder in your area could not do an acceptable job for you if he did not know his business. The honest, intelligent builder who does not yet know all the answers is more likely to admit that, and seek advice from others.

How do you find this knowledgeable, honest builder? Ask other people. Good news travels fast; bad news even more quickly (everyone has, or knows about, a housing horror story). If you are planning to have a house built in a subdivision, ask the people already living there about the builder. Did he make all the little repairs and corrections they requested? Many builders will make the big, obvious corrections, but will never quite get around to the small problems. Only a very conscientious builder will repair or replace the little things reasonably promptly and reasonably pleasantly.

What kind of small detail? In a new house, the buyer is entitled to a replacement electrical outlet cover if one is broken, as well as replacements for any broken window panes. The need for any repairs, major and minor, should be clearly stated in writing on what is known as a buyer's "Punch Out List".

The number of houses that a builder can build in a year has little relationship to the quality of the workmanship or materials. Large national home building companies set the standards for the types of materials and equipment used in their houses. However, this does not mean that the quality is better. These standards only mean that all the houses are the same, complying in a uniform way to their own standards. A small or one-at-a-time builder may or may not build to higher standards.

Some builders offer a ten year structural warranty on new homes, through homeowners' warranty programs. Limited warranties may be available on resale houses. Houses warranted under these programs must comply with certain requirements and the houses are warranted only under certain circumstances. There is a booklet available to explain the specifics of these warranty programs. The warranty is similar to insurance; you hope you never need it, but if the need arises you are covered.

Large home building companies, especially those that are publicly held, focus first on their profit. If they can find a way to save five hundred dollars per house by making a few changes in material (without negatively affecting the appearance of the house) they probably will do so. Labor costs can be trimmed similarly; using three nails to a board instead of four can add up to a significant saving for a large builder. Most larger home building companies give good value, but may not contribute the "bonus" values you are more apt to get from an independent contractor.

Being an informed, responsible home buyer is almost a civic responsibility. The home buyer who has not done his "home" work and buys a house of inferior quality must share some of the responsibility for all the poor quality homes that are built. The individual who buys the "glitter" without checking the structure of the house is particularly at fault. Builders understand that this kind of buyer is, unfortunately, in the majority. Accordingly, they will cut every corner possible until they get to the finishing items, then decorate the house with wallpaper, molding, garden tubs, etc. so the house looks terrific. Then the buyer makes what he thinks is an "apples to apples" comparison with another house — where the builder put his money into quality construction materials, not paint and paper — and buys the house with the more visible, cosmetic appeal.

Because the structure of the house purchased is not nearly as good as the house disdained, the buyer is the eventual loser. Some builders say this is not a problem; the average home buyer can't tell the difference anyway and besides, they are giving the buyer what he wants. And maybe this is so. Unfortunately, particularly for the owner who plans to stay indefinitely in the house he has just bought, the less fancy, but better built house would have been the better buy. The home owner can always add wallpaper or install track lighting as he wishes and the budget permits. The monthly mortgage payment should be paying for quality construction; meat and potatoes, not garnishes.

Builders and real estate agents say there is no such thing as a perfect house. And that's true. With all the variables involved in building and finishing a house, you are not apt to find one that is exactly right for you. The best way to find a good builder is to inspect and evaluate houses he has built — after you have made yourself a knowledgeable home buyer and understand what it is you are inspecting. The information in this book should qualify you.

THE REAL ESTATE AGENT

The person who approaches you in a subdivision and asks if he or she can show you some of the houses is not always a real estate agent. Many times the builder has a sales representative who works exclusively for him. This representative may not be affiliated with any real estate agency. Also, he or she may not have any industry guidelines to follow or professional requirements to satisfy. However, most builders, builder's representatives, and real estate agents are honest. As the prospective buyer, it is your responsibility to ask the right questions, no matter who the sales person is.

Both the real estate agent and the builder's representative are working for the builder on a commission basis, so their loyalty is to him. Even when a real estate agent shows a resale house, his loyalty is to the seller. In some states, laws are being implemented that require real estate agents to make known the fact that they represent the seller, and to treat the buyers in an honest, fair, and accurate manner in response to all questions concerning the house. Here again, the burden of asking the right questions belongs to the buyer.

Real estate agents are good sources for houses being shown by other agents, as well as for mortgages and other financial information. Most real estate companies and builders will "co-op" with other company's agents. One company is offering the house for sale but another company sells it, so the companies split the commission. Therefore, it is not necessary to keep changing agents to look at houses your agent does not list. You are better off dealing with one agent who knows the area, knows what you want, and knows construction.

If you feel uncomfortable with one agent, for whatever reason, look for another. No area or community has the problem of too few real estate agents. As the one who must decide if a particular house is a good buy, you have some leverage. Exercise that leverage by being sure to include in the contract that any repairs will be completed prior to the closing. If that is not acceptable, make an offer minus the cost of the repairs. Be reasonable, know what you are talking about, and don't expect every tiny nick or scratch to be fixed. Remember, the perfect house does not exist. However, all the items check-listed in this book are reasonable and fair. This is especially true if you are buying an expensive home. If you have negotiated a price reduction, realize that a compromise has been reached. It would not be fair to expect all the minor repairs to be made if you have agreed to a settlement that, in effect, puts the "repair ball" back in your court.

SUMMARY

This book was researched, compiled, and written to give you, the prospective homebuyer, adequate knowledge of construction methods and materials, an awareness of the problems that can develop during the construction process, and an understanding of the causes and effects of, and cures for, those problems. Once you have read this book and familiarized yourself with the inspection checklists, you will be an "educated home buyer". You will be in a better position to pick the house that is best suited for you, in all respects. However, the proper use of the checklists is important. If you are in doubt about any item, professional guidance is strongly recommended.

Checklist #7: Built-in Appliances and Interior/Exterior Amenities

	House #1 Location:_____	NO PROBLEM	MINIMUM	MINOR	MAJOR	HOLD
		0	1	2	3	?
1	Does the kitchen equipment function properly?					
2	Will any kitchen appliance need to be replaced?					
3	Kitchen appliance replacement: Is the model still available?					
4	Is the owner pleased with the dishwasher's performance?					
5	Kitchen Extras? Are they working?					
6	Garbage Disposal: Is it connected to sewer? To septic system?					
7	Swimming Pool: Has it been maintained properly?					
8	Swimming Pool: Does it need major repairs?					
9	Pool Decking: Is it intact and safe?					
10	Fencing around pool area? Around perimeter of property? Is it in good condition?					
11	Fireplace: Is the chimney placement correct for proper drafting?					
12	Fireplace: Does it draft properly?					
13	Fireplace: Has the chase been cleaned out on a regular basis?					
14	Wood Burning Stove: Do you see any signs of past problems?					
15	Is there a Community Recreation Area? Is it well maintained?					
16	REMARKS OR OTHER:					
17						
18						
19						
20						
21						
22						
23						
24						
25						
26						
27						
28						
29						
30						

TRANSFER SUB-TOTALS TO
MASTER CHECKLIST FORM

SUB-TOTAL

ADDITIONAL REMARKS OR OTHERS:

Checklist #7: Built-in Appliances and Interior/Exterior Amenities

	House #2　　Location:_____	NO PROBLEM	MINIMUM	MINOR	MAJOR	HOLD
		0	1	2	3	?
1	Does the kitchen equipment function properly?					
2	Will any kitchen appliance need to be replaced?					
3	Kitchen appliance replacement: Is the model still available?					
4	Is the owner pleased with the dishwasher's performance?					
5	Kitchen Extras? Are they working?					
6	Garbage Disposal: Is it connected to sewer? To septic system?					
7	Swimming Pool: Has it been maintained properly?					
8	Swimming Pool: Does it need major repairs?					
9	Pool Decking: Is it intact and safe?					
10	Fencing around pool area? Around perimeter of property? Is it in good condition?					
11	Fireplace: Is the chimney placement correct for proper drafting?					
12	Fireplace: Does it draft properly?					
13	Fireplace: Has the chase been cleaned out on a regular basis?					
14	Wood Burning Stove: Do you see any signs of past problems?					
15	Is there a Community Recreation Area? Is it well maintained?					
16	REMARKS OR OTHER:					
17						
18						
19						
20						
21						
22						
23						
24						
25						
26						
27						
28						
29						
30						
	SUB-TOTAL					

TRANSFER SUB-TOTALS TO
MASTER CHECKLIST FORM

ADDITIONAL REMARKS OR OTHERS:

Checklist #7: Built-in Appliances and Interior/Exterior Amenities

	House #3 Location:_____	NO PROBLEM	MINIMUM	MINOR	MAJOR	HOLD
		0	1	2	3	?
1	Does the kitchen equipment function properly?					
2	Will any kitchen appliance need to be replaced?					
3	Kitchen appliance replacement: Is the model still available?					
4	Is the owner pleased with the dishwasher's performance?					
5	Kitchen Extras? Are they working?					
6	Garbage Disposal: Is it connected to sewer? To septic system?					
7	Swimming Pool: Has it been maintained properly?					
8	Swimming Pool: Does it need major repairs?					
9	Pool Decking: Is it intact and safe?					
10	Fencing around pool area? Around perimeter of property? Is it in good condition?					
11	Fireplace: Is the chimney placement correct for proper drafting?					
12	Fireplace: Does it draft properly?					
13	Fireplace: Has the chase been cleaned out on a regular basis?					
14	Wood Burning Stove: Do you see any signs of past problems?					
15	Is there a Community Recreation Area? Is it well maintained?					
16	REMARKS OR OTHER:					
17						
18						
19						
20						
21						
22						
23						
24						
25						
26						
27						
28						
29						
30						

TRANSFER SUB-TOTALS TO
MASTER CHECKLIST FORM

| SUB-TOTAL | | | | |

ADDITIONAL REMARKS OR OTHERS:

Explanation For Use Of Master Checklist

The Master Checklist can be your guide to comparing two or more houses or a tool enabling you to evaluate one house very carefully. You will want to add up the scores from each chapter-ending checklist. Before doing that, however, you need to investigate any "Hold" entries that were checked. Investigation will enable you to assign that entry a score.

Next, these subtotals are transferred to the Master Checklist, each score listed by the appropriate checklist number. Then the subtotals are multiplied by the number assigned to the severity of the problem (1: Minimum, 2: Minor, 3: Major). This will give you the "Totals" to enter. These then are added to obtain the "Grand Total". The "No Problem" column merely indicates the items that are free of problems, and does not contribute to the Grand Total. The prospective home buyer is advised to be extremely cautious about committing to any house scored with a number of minor problems or more than one major problem. Even one major structural problem is cause for extreme caution. For additional guidance, look at the sample Master Checklist on the following page.

Master Checklist

House #1 Location: _____	N O P R O B L E M 0	M I N I M U M 1	M I N O R 2	M A J O R 3
CHECKLIST NUMBER #1				
CHECKLIST NUMBER #2				
CHECKLIST NUMBER #3				
CHECKLIST NUMBER #4				
CHECKLIST NUMBER #5				
CHECKLIST NUMBER #6				
CHECKLIST NUMBER #7				
SUB-TOTAL OF COL. M-1, M-2, M-3				
TOTAL OF COL. M-1X1, M-2X2, M-3X3 =				
GRAND TOTAL OF COL. M-1, M-2, M-3				

Remarks Checklist #1 _____

_____

Remarks Checklist #2 _____

_____

Remarks Checklist #3 _____

_____

Remarks Checklist #4 _____

_____

Remarks Checklist #5 _____

_____

Remarks Checklist #6 _____

_____

Remarks Checklist #7 _____

_____

ADDITIONAL REMARKS OR OTHERS:

_____

_____

_____

_____

_____

_____

_____

_____

_____

_____

_____

_____

_____

_____

Master Checklist

House #2 Location: _____	NO PROBLEM 0	MINIMUM 1	MINOR 2	MAJOR 3
CHECKLIST NUMBER #1				
CHECKLIST NUMBER #2				
CHECKLIST NUMBER #3				
CHECKLIST NUMBER #4				
CHECKLIST NUMBER #5				
CHECKLIST NUMBER #6				
CHECKLIST NUMBER #7				
SUB-TOTAL OF COL. M-1, M-2, M-3				
TOTAL OF COL. M-1X1, M-2X2, M-3X3 =				
GRAND TOTAL OF COL. M-1, M-2, M-3				

Remarks Checklist #1
_____
_____

Remarks Checklist #2
_____
_____

Remarks Checklist #3
_____
_____

Remarks Checklist #4
_____
_____

Remarks Checklist #5
_____
_____

Remarks Checklist #6
_____
_____

Remarks Checklist #7
_____
_____

ADDITIONAL REMARKS OR OTHERS:

_____

_____

_____

_____

_____

_____

_____

_____

_____

_____

_____

_____

_____

_____

_____

_____

_____

Master Checklist

House #3 Location: _____	NO PROBLEM 0	MINIMUM 1	MINOR 2	MAJOR 3
CHECKLIST NUMBER #1				
CHECKLIST NUMBER #2				
CHECKLIST NUMBER #3				
CHECKLIST NUMBER #4				
CHECKLIST NUMBER #5				
CHECKLIST NUMBER #6				
CHECKLIST NUMBER #7				
SUB-TOTAL OF COL. M-1, M-2, M-3				
TOTAL OF COL. M-1X1, M-2X2, M-3X3 =				
GRAND TOTAL OF COL. M-1, M-2, M-3				

Remarks Checklist #1 _____
_____

Remarks Checklist #2 _____
_____

Remarks Checklist #3 _____
_____

Remarks Checklist #4 _____
_____

Remarks Checklist #5 _____
_____

Remarks Checklist #6 _____
_____

Remarks Checklist #7 _____
_____
_____

ADDITIONAL REMARKS OR OTHERS:

Explanation For Use Of The "Quick" Checklist

The Quick Checklist is a summary of the most important questions that have been asked on the other checklists. For example, questions 18 & 19 on the checklist concern dangerous electrical situations and the need to rewire the entire house; the kind of problem that should induce the prudent home buyer to look for housing elsewhere (unless a substantial price concession compensates for the problem).

A number of "one point" problems should raise serious questions about the suitability of the house. One "three point" problem probably is sufficient reason to look elsewhere.

After each question, you will see a number in brackets. This number refers to the chapter in which further information on this subject can be found.

Quick Checklist

	House #1 Location:_____		NO PROBLEM 0	MINIMUM 1	MINOR 2	MAJOR 3	HOLD ?
1	Does the lot and/or house have drainage problems?	[1]					
2	Excessive number of resales in the area?	[1]					
3	Is there a vertical foundation crack that is largest at the top?	[2]					
4	Does the house have foundation and floor problems? THINK TWICE	[2]					
5	Will the roof require repair? New Roofing?	[2]					
6	Does the house have excessive water stains? Wood rot?	[3]					
7	Do you see any bows in a brick or stucco wall?	[3]					
8	Are there any stress or settlement cracks in a brick or rock wall?	[3]					
9	Stucco siding: Are there patch spots in the stucco?	[3]					
10	Wood siding: Do you see split siding? In an isolated area?	[3]					
11	Hardboard siding: Are any boards cracked?	[3]					
12	Do you see water damage at the roof line?	[3]					
13	Septic Tank: Have there been past problems with it?	[4]					
14	Will you need to tap into sewer? Is sewer available?	[4]					
15	Are all water pipes in satisfactory condition?	[4]					
16	Have there been any problems with the drainlines and/or drainage?	[4]					
17	Are the present utility bills acceptable for your budget?	[4]					
18	Are there indications that the house may need rewiring?	[4]					
19	Are any fuses or circuit breakers warm to the touch? DANGER	[4]					
20	Is there evidence of past overloading of lighting fixtures?	[4]					
21	Do you see any color changes in the roofing?	[5]					
22	Is the roof turning up at the edge, cracking or blistering?	[5]					
23	Are there cracks in the sheetrock? WARNING: May be structural	[5]					
24	Do the ceilings droop or appear to roll?	[5]					
25	Does the outside of the house need repainting?	[6]					
26	Do you think that any inside paint is hiding a problem?	[6]					
27	Are the carpets in good condition? Replacement soon?	[6]					
28	Will you need to repair any flooring?	[6]					
29	Will any kitchen appliance need to be replaced?	[7]					
30	Fireplace: Is the chimney placement correct for proper drafting?	[7]					
		TOTAL					

ADDITIONAL REMARKS OR OTHERS:

_____

_____

_____

_____

_____

_____

_____

_____

_____

_____

_____

_____

_____

_____

Quick Checklist

	House #2 Location:_____		NO PROBLEM 0	MINIMUM 1	MINOR 2	MAJOR 3	HOLD ?
1	Does the lot and/or house have drainage problems?	[1]					
2	Excessive number of resales in the area?	[1]					
3	Is there a vertical foundation crack that is largest at the top?	[2]					
4	Does the house have foundation and floor problems? THINK TWICE	[2]					
5	Will the roof require repair? New Roofing?	[2]					
6	Does the house have excessive water stains? Wood rot?	[3]					
7	Do you see any bows in a brick or stucco wall?	[3]					
8	Are there any stress or settlement cracks in a brick or rock wall?	[3]					
9	Stucco siding: Are there patch spots in the stucco?	[3]					
10	Wood siding: Do you see split siding? In an isolated area?	[3]					
11	Hardboard siding: Are any boards cracked?	[3]					
12	Do you see water damage at the roof line?	[3]					
13	Septic Tank: Have there been past problems with it?	[4]					
14	Will you need to tap into sewer? Is sewer available?	[4]					
15	Are all water pipes in satisfactory condition?	[4]					
16	Have there been any problems with the drainlines and/or drainage?	[4]					
17	Are the present utility bills acceptable for your budget?	[4]					
18	Are there indications that the house may need rewiring?	[4]					
19	Are any fuses or circuit breakers warm to the touch? DANGER	[4]					
20	Is there evidence of past overloading of lighting fixtures?	[4]					
21	Do you see any color changes in the roofing?	[5]					
22	Is the roof turning up at the edge, cracking or blistering?	[5]					
23	Are there cracks in the sheetrock? WARNING: May be structural	[5]					
24	Do the ceilings droop or appear to roll?	[5]					
25	Does the outside of the house need repainting?	[6]					
26	Do you think that any inside paint is hiding a problem?	[6]					
27	Are the carpets in good condition? Replacement soon?	[6]					
28	Will you need to repair any flooring?	[6]					
29	Will any kitchen appliance need to be replaced?	[7]					
30	Fireplace: Is the chimney placement correct for proper drafting?	[7]					
		TOTAL					

ADDITIONAL REMARKS OR OTHERS:

Quick Checklist

	House #3 Location:_____		NO PROBLEM 0	MINIMUM 1	MINOR 2	MAJOR 3	HOLD ?
1	Does the lot and/or house have drainage problems?	[1]					
2	Excessive number of resales in the area?	[1]					
3	Is there a vertical foundation crack that is largest at the top?	[2]					
4	Does the house have foundation and floor problems? THINK TWICE	[2]					
5	Will the roof require repair? New Roofing?	[2]					
6	Does the house have excessive water stains? Wood rot?	[3]					
7	Do you see any bows in a brick or stucco wall?	[3]					
8	Are there any stress or settlement cracks in a brick or rock wall?	[3]					
9	Stucco siding: Are there patch spots in the stucco?	[3]					
10	Wood siding: Do you see split siding? In an isolated area?	[3]					
11	Hardboard siding: Are any boards cracked?	[3]					
12	Do you see water damage at the roof line?	[3]					
13	Septic Tank: Have there been past problems with it?	[4]					
14	Will you need to tap into sewer? Is sewer available?	[4]					
15	Are all water pipes in satisfactory condition?	[4]					
16	Have there been any problems with the drainlines and/or drainage?	[4]					
17	Are the present utility bills acceptable for your budget?	[4]					
18	Are there indications that the house may need rewiring?	[4]					
19	Are any fuses or circuit breakers warm to the touch? DANGER	[4]					
20	Is there evidence of past overloading of lighting fixtures?	[4]					
21	Do you see any color changes in the roofing?	[5]					
22	Is the roof turning up at the edge, cracking or blistering?	[5]					
23	Are there cracks in the sheetrock? WARNING: May be structural	[5]					
24	Do the ceilings droop or appear to roll?	[5]					
25	Does the outside of the house need repainting?	[6]					
26	Do you think that any inside paint is hiding a problem?	[6]					
27	Are the carpets in good condition? Replacement soon?	[6]					
28	Will you need to repair any flooring?	[6]					
29	Will any kitchen appliance need to be replaced?	[7]					
30	Fireplace: Is the chimney placement correct for proper drafting?	[7]					
	TOTAL						

ADDITIONAL REMARKS OR OTHERS:

_____

_____

_____

_____

_____

_____

_____

_____

_____

_____

_____

_____

_____

_____

Index